Looking Afresh

Hugh Montefiore, former Bishop of Birmingham, is the
author of many books on Christianity.

Looking Afresh

Soundings in Creative Dissent

HUGH MONTEFIORE

First published in Great Britain in 2002 by
Society for Promoting Christian Knowledge
Holy Trinity Church
Marylebone Road
London NW1 4DU

British Library Cataloguing-in-Publication Data
A catalogue record for this book is available from the British Library

ISBN 0-281-05537-8

10 9 8 7 6 5 4 3 2 1

Typeset by FiSH Books, London.
Printed in Great Britain by Antony Rowe Ltd, Chippenham, Wiltshire

Contents

Preface

The essays included here are, many of them, second thoughts, near the end of a long ministry. There is nothing wrong in second thoughts: they may well be better than first thoughts. The search for truth is all important, and fresh insights, even if they may involve abandoning earlier positions, ought always to be welcomed.

I realize that these may sometimes be controversial. Again, there is nothing wrong in that: after all, Jesus Christ could be exceedingly controversial. I do not expect everyone to agree with me, but there should be room in the Church for views which at the moment may not be always acceptable. I remain, I hope, a loyal Anglican. If some regard old age as redolent of senility, happily there is another line of thought which regards it as the repository of wisdom.

Some of these themes have been taken from recent lectures, and two from a recent publication.

Hugh Montefiore

1

Overdefinition in Doctrine

Until the advent of *Common Worship*, the Church of England was the most credalized in all Christendom. In its Prayer Book the Apostles' Creed is said in its Morning and Evening Prayer, and in its Eucharist the so-called Nicene Creed is recited, Sunday after Sunday. In this there are said or sung the words:

We believe in one Lord, Jesus Christ,
the only Son of God,
eternally begotten of the Father,
God from God, Light from Light,
true God from true God,
begotten, not made,
of one Being with the Father;
through him all things were made...

Greater still definition can be found elsewhere. The classic statement of orthodoxy concerning the person of Christ is found in what is known as the Chalcedonian Definition of AD 451:

Following the Holy Fathers, we all with one voice teach that it should be confessed that our Lord Jesus Christ is one and the same Son, the Same complete in godhead, the Same complete in humanity, truly God, and truly man, the Same of a rational soul and body, of one substance with the Father as touching his manhood, and of one substance with us as touching his humanity, in all respects like us sin alone excepted, begotten of the Father before all ages as touching his godhead, and, in the last days, the Same, for us men and for our salvation, of Mary the Virgin the Mother of God as to his humanity, one and the same Christ, Son, Lord, Only Begotten, made known in two natures without confusion, without change, without division, without separation, the difference of the natures being in no way taken away by reason of the union, but rather the properties of each being preserved, and both concurring into the one person and substance, not divided or parted into two persons and substances...

This somewhat indigestible and tortured definition is evidently an academic statement unsuited to general use. It was developed from one of the creeds.

It is not my intention in what follows to criticize these statements about the person of Christ (which are considered orthodox by most Christian Churches) on the grounds that they are wrong. They may be right. I want only to ask questions about their suitability, and to suggest that they overdefine Christian doctrine, in the sense that they go beyond what can properly be said.

To examine the credentials of the Nicene-Constantinopolitan Creed, which stems from the ecumenical council of Nicaea in AD 325, it is necessary to consider the circumstances in which it was produced. After Constantine had won control of the Roman Empire, although he was himself unbaptized, he adopted the Christian faith for his Empire. Thereafter, when weighty matters of doctrine were being resolved, church councils were strongly under the influence of the Emperor. The First Ecumenical Council of AD 325, although it is called ecumenical, in fact had only five bishops from the West present. But the Emperor was there; and the same could be said of similar councils held during the reigns of Constantine's successors.

As noted above, we affirm in the Nicene Creed that Christ is 'of one Being with the Father' (or 'of one substance with the Father' in an older translation). The Greek word here, *homoousios*, is not found in Scripture, and in that sense it could be said that the Creed is unscriptural. This would at first sight seem to be a real objection; but if our belief is to be expressed in contemporary language, then we must allow that this is just what the Council attempted to do in respect of the *homoousios*. But it was a phrase little known in the early Church, and those who had used it were suspect theologians. It had been employed by Valentinus, who had been adjudged a heretic. It had also been used by Paul of Samosata, regarded with the deepest suspicion by the early Fathers.

Why then was it included in the Creed? The historian Leitzmann asserted that it was due to the 'amateurish theology of the Emperor, supported by the immeasurable prestige of his status' (Leitzmann, 1961, p. 119). Today this is generally regarded as an overstatement. Yet undoubtedly the Emperor carried great weight. For centuries the Church had been subject, on and off, to savage persecution by the Roman emperors, or they had stood aloof when local persecutions took place. Instead of rulers who distrusted or hated Christians, they now had one who was actually in favour of the Church and who wanted it united so that it could help to cement the Empire. Furthermore, accounts of the Council speak of the pomp surrounding the Emperor's attendance and the importance given to his presence. Yet, for all his influence, he was as yet unbaptized, and not even a catechumen. The situation was not wholly unlike that of the reformation of the Church of England when Henry VIII persuaded the English authorities to renounce papal authority, except that the king had no intention of changing or redefining Christian doctrine, and he had been baptized and confirmed. Of course the fact that *homoousios*, the key word in the Creed, was greatly influenced by the Emperor's wishes does not in itself mean that it was inappropriate; but it does raise questions about its suitability.

If *homoousios* is not found in the New Testament, we must ask whether 'of one Being with the Father' properly represents the New Testament teaching about Christ. The first priority is to determine whether the phrase encapsulates Jesus's own teaching about himself. It certainly is consonant with one of his sayings reported in St John's Gospel. We find: 'I and my Father are one' (John 10.30), although the neuter form *hen* is used here ('one thing', even 'at one') rather than *heis* which would mean that Jesus and his Heavenly Father are literally one. Against this might be cited the beginning of St John's Gospel, where it is said that the Word was *theos*, not *ho theos* with the definite article as would be expected if the author intended to equate the Word with God himself, rather than merely to affirm the divinity of the Word. However, it is unsafe to quote texts from the Fourth Gospel as though they come from the lips of Jesus. Although the work certainly contains genuine historical reminiscences, it is also generally agreed to be to a large extent a meditation about Jesus, and it is difficult sometimes to determine where Jesus's words end, and the author's reflections begin.

If we are looking for what Jesus actually said, it is safer to consider sayings found in the Synoptic Gospels. There, when a rich young man calls Jesus 'Good master', he responds with the words 'Why do you call me good? Nobody is good save only God' (Mark 10.18). This does not explicitly deny that Jesus is God, but it is certainly implicit in the reply. It is inconceivable that it is a later invention, for no one would have made up a sentence which might appear to diminish the status of Jesus; so much so, that in the later St Matthew's Gospel the reply is somewhat softened to 'Why do you ask me concerning that which is good?' (Matthew 19.17). If a person calls someone 'Your Grace' and is met with the reply 'Why do you call me Your Grace? Only archbishops are called that', he would immediately infer that the addressee wished to make clear that he is not an archbishop. Similarly. with his response to the rich young man, Jesus seems to go out of his way to disclaim being God. Those who espouse 'kenotic Christology' (the view that Christ emptied himself of divinity in becoming man) might claim that he did not know himself as God, although in fact he was. To say nothing of the difficulties involved in kenoticism, such a claim is remarkably unconvincing. It is hard to imagine God denying that he is God!

Jesus showed extreme reserve about accepting the title Messiah, preferring the enigmatic Son of Man. Similarly he showed reserve in claiming that he was Lord (in the full sense of the word as expressive of God), although he certainly accepted it in the sense of 'Sir' (Matthew 7.21; Mark 11.3). At the same time he was deeply conscious that he had a very special place in God's dispensation, and a divine vocation to inaugurate God's kingdom (Matthew 13.16–17, 12.28). Did Jesus ever refer to himself as the Son of God? If we accept St John's Gospel as containing throughout the actual words of Jesus, the answer must be 'Yes'; but we have already rejected this approach. There is also in two of the Synoptic Gospels the strange passage: 'No man knows the Son but the Father; nor does anyone know the Father save the Son and he to whomsoever the Son reveals him (Matthew. 11.27; Luke 10.22). It is possible that these words were spoken by Jesus, but the absolute use of Son (rather than Son of God) suggests that they have been influenced by post-resurrection tradition, like the baptism formula at the end of St Matthew's Gospel.

From this brief survey it seems that the use of the word *homoousios* probably does not reflect Jesus's own views about himself. But what of the rest of the New Testament, consisting of letters written after Jesus's death and resurrection?

Here the titles of Lord, Christ and Son of God are freely used to describe the risen Jesus. As Peter is reported as saying at the first Pentecost: 'Let all the house of Israel assuredly know that God has made that same Jesus, whom you crucified, both Lord and Christ' (Acts 2.36). However there are only two occasions (other than John 1.1, discussed above) when Jesus in the New Testament is explicitly called God. One of these concerns

Thomas, who, when he saw the risen Jesus, exclaimed 'My Lord and my God' (John 20.28). Once again, caution should be used in taking statements in that Gospel as reporting the *ipsissima verba* of Jesus.

The second affirmation of Jesus as God is found in Hebrews 1.9. This Epistle, with its strong emphasis on the humanity of Jesus, has also the highest Christology in the New Testament. Here, in the first chapter, the author (whoever he may have been) used the Jewish psalms to attest the person of Jesus, contrasting him with the angels. He cites from Psalm 45.6 (AV) which he rather strangely assumes to refer to the Son: 'Thy throne, O God, is for ever and ever', and continues up to the words: 'Therefore God, thy God, hath anointed thee with the oil of gladness above thy fellows'. Certainly the author intended here to ascribe divinity to Jesus, but it may be doubted whether he meant more than that.

Even if all these texts do refer to the full divinity of Jesus, it can hardly be said that three New Testament references afford a strong justification for the use of *homoousios*. Certainly Lord, Word and Son of God are freely used in the Epistles and the Acts to refer to Jesus, but it must be remembered that these were ambiguous in meaning. Both in Jewish and in Hellenistic writings they can be freely used to attribute far less than full divinity.

One of the more interesting statements of New Testament Christology is to be found in the Epistle to the Philippians. There Christ Jesus is said to have been (in his preincarnate existence) not God but 'in the form of God' (Philippians 2.6); in other words, divine. We are told that he thought it not *harpasmos* to be on equality with God, but took the form of servant, and was made in the likeness of men. *Harpasmos* is derived from the Greek verb *harpazein*, to snatch or to seize. So it can hardly mean that Jesus did not want to cling on to equality with God: on the contrary, it means that he did not want to snatch it for himself, but he preferred to take the form of a servant. It was because of this amazing act of humility that, after Jesus had become obedient to death, God 'exalted him and gave him a name above every other name, that at the name of Jesus every knee should bow and every tongue confess that Jesus Christ is Lord to the glory of God the Father'. Paul does not say here that the risen Jesus was God after his resurrection, but he does say that thereafter he is to be worshipped and adored as Lord; in other words, he is divine. It is hard to use this passage to justify the phrases of the Creed 'eternally begotten of the Father' and 'of one Being with the Father'.

To sum up, the New Testament tells us that Jesus in his earthly life inaugurated God's kingdom, that the risen Jesus is to be worshipped, that he is divine, that he reveals to us the nature of God, but not that he is of one substance with the Father. As Cullmann wrote:

> The fundamental answer to the question whether the New Testament teaches Christ's 'deity' is therefore 'Yes'. But to this 'yes' we must further add: 'on condition we do not connect the concept with later Greek speculations about substance and natures, but understand it strictly from the standpoint of *Heilsgeschichte*. Without a divine *Heilsgeschichte* it would not make sense to speak of Jesus' deity. He would then simply be one of the heroes of history – nothing more. Conversely it would likewise be senseless without *Heilsgeschichte* to distinguish God the Father from the Logos, his revelation, his 'Son'. (Cullmann, 1959, p. 306)

The fact that we cannot read 'of one Being with the Father' out of the New Testament does not mean that it may not be true, and there will certainly be those who believe that this is the case. But it does suggest that it is a pity to tie orthodox Christian belief to this formula. For this reason I am not suggesting that the Nicene Creed no longer be used in the worship of the Church. But I do suggest that there should be an alternative Creed which could be used at the discretion of the minister with the approval of the authorities of the local church. It might be modelled on the ancient Creed of Caesarea which was put forward by Eusebius but rejected at the Council of Nicaea. Although I believe that the Church is primarily a fellowship of those who love the Lord Jesus and who are his followers, some credal statements are needed, as necessary safeguards for the Churches. To affirm that God is too mysterious for us to say anything about him is intellectually sloppy and pastorally calamitous. At the same time it could be the case that certain doctrines, especially those about Christ's person, have been overdefined.

Some 130 years after the Council of Nicaea, another Council was summoned to meet there in order to settle outstanding christological problems. The venue was later changed to Chalcedon, so that the Empress Pulcheria's husband could attend. As with many Councils, there was a hidden agenda. In this case it was the Empress who wanted to assert the supremacy of Constantinople over the rival see of Alexandria. The resulting 'Chalcedonian Definition', cited above, was built upon the Nicene Creed, but gave further precision to what had been earlier asserted. The Definition, which has been regarded as the final definition of christological orthodoxy, affirmed the unity of Christ's person, the reality and permanence of each nature, human and divine, and the relationship of the two natures which were united in one person 'without confusion, without change, without division, without separation'. There was no explanation about whether such a union of natures is possible, or indeed what it would mean if it had come about.

What would be the loss and gain of such a move? It is claimed that these formulae have protected Churches from error. This may be the case. It is not suggested here that these formulations should be abolished, but that in addition to the traditional Nicene Creed, there should also be one that does not include the *homoousios*.

Some might feel that Christianity would lose its way unless the person of Christ were defined precisely in the traditional orthodox manner. Yet the fourth-century Ulphilas, who lived in Edessa, held Arian beliefs (e.g. that Christ was created rather than eternal); but this did not prevent him from converting the Goths from heathenism, and there is even a fragmentary confession of faith written in Arian terms which he wrote for the Goths, who formed the greater part of the Western Roman Empire. Arian Christianity was a missionary faith. No loss of cutting edge there!

Again, it is claimed that when a doctrine has been defined by an Ecumenical Council, this ends bickering and unites the Church. Putting aside the question whether the Council of Nicaea was genuinely ecumenical such a view is contradicted by the facts. The Nicene Creed formed the basis of the longer Chalcedonian Definition. This was accepted by an Ecumenical Council, and has become part of orthodoxy. But it certainly did not put an end to bickering or promote the unity of the Church. Indeed it was the cause of schism in the early Church. Monophysitism, the doctrine that the incarnate Christ had not two natures but one nature, lived on after Chalcedon and is still alive today in Syria, Armenia and Ethiopia. (However, unofficial meetings between the Eastern Orthodox and Oriental Churches in the 1960s and 1970s concluded that the differences between monophysites and those who accepted Chalcedon were terminological rather than theological (Gregorios *et al.*, 1981). Nonetheless these differences led to schism.) The Nestorian Church, following Nestorius, Patriarch of Constantinople (who taught that the divine and human natures of Christ were distinct and merely conjoined) spread to Persia, India and even China, and in the tenth and eleventh centuries became the largest Church in Christendom. It cannot be maintained that strict traditional orthodoxy is necessary either for missionary success or for ecclesiastical unity.

Dissatisfaction with the Chalcedonian Definition, together with a reluctance to use the fourth-century terminology of nature and substance, has led to many attempts to explain Christology with the use of other models and paradigms. A great number of books have been written on the subject. Some models are more satisfying than others, although none are without their problems. In the first essay that I ever published, in a contribution to *Soundings* (ed. Vidler, 1963, pp. 149–72), I suggested the substitution of the concept of the pattern of divine activity for the divine substance of Christ. Writing considerably later, I tried to show that the categories of grace or of the Holy Spirit can help to explain the relationship of Christ to his Heavenly Father (Montefiore, 1993, pp. 88ff.). Neither of these suggestions was totally satisfactory. Perhaps we should admit that, if God expressed himself fully in terms of humanity in so far as humanity is capable of expressing him, we shall never be able fully to define the person of Christ, because we do not know enough about the nature of God. It must be sufficient to affirm that Jesus not merely was fully human, but also that God used him to reveal himself through human personality in a way which no mere man could do; and so he is divine.

No doubt it will be objected that such a conclusion lacks intellectual depth, and that it weakens the Christian faith. But the Church has never defined the doctrine of the atonement. It has been sufficient to declare that the incarnation took place 'for us men and for our salvation' without any explanation about how this came about. Of course the New Testament Scriptures contain many images and metaphors to convey the reality of the atonement. Furthermore individual Christian theologians have produced their own doctrines of the atonement, either by the expansion of one of these metaphors, or by the use of some other imagery. But the Church has never endorsed any particular doctrine. I do not think that it can be plausibly argued that this has weakened the Christian faith. In contrast to the doctrine of the atonement, Christology seems greatly overdeveloped, due to the concern of the early Church with Hellenistic metaphysics. Comparison with the doctrine of the atonement suggests that greater flexibility about the doctrine would not depreciate the Christian faith.

If there has been overdefinition of doctrine in the case of Christology, this has important implications for the doctrine of the Holy Trinity. According to orthodox doctrine, there are three persons and one God. We tend to understand this as attributing to God three separate personalities, since the modern use of the word 'person' is very different in meaning from the Greek and Latin words used in the early Church to describe the mystery of God. In Latin the word *persona* meant primarily a mask. *Hypostasis* and *ousia* were the most frequently used terms in Greek. 'There is *mia ousia* and *treis hypostaseis*, or *mia ousia en trisin hypostasin* – one substance or essence or entity, in three subsistencies or forms or modes of existence or consciousness; one God permanently existing in one and the same' (Bethune-Baker, 1961, p. 238).

In Holy Scripture there is only one reference to a heavenly Trinity, and no reference whatever to the eternal relationships of the three persons. The First Epistle of St John has:

> There are three that bear record in heaven, the Father, the Word, and the Holy Ghost, and these three are one. And there are three that bear witness on earth, the Spirit, and the water, and the blood; and these three agree in one. (1 John 5.7–8)

This seems a weak basis on which to build that which has been described as the core of the Christian faith. The 'three that bear record in heaven, the Father, the Word, and the Holy Ghost' is found in the Western manuscripts and in Latin Fathers, but not in the main ancient texts, and it is not included in the Greek text of Nestlé, or even in the English of the New English Bible: it is very unlikely to have been part of the original text. There are many references, chiefly in St John's Gospel, to the fact that God reveals himself to humankind in three modes. (Such a belief is different from the Patripassian heresy, according to which there is no distinction between the three persons of the Trinity, so that the Father was crucified on the cross.) But the traditional doctrine of the Trinity is much more far-reaching than a statement about how God reveals himself. It makes an assertion about the eternal nature of the Triune God. This is sometimes called 'the essential Trinity', in contrast to 'the economic Trinity' according to which God reveals himself to humankind in three modes. But we have no knowledge of God whatsoever as he is in himself. We only know what he reveals to us. We know nothing about any interior relationship within the godhead. It may be objected that God would not deceive us: he is bound to reveal himself to humankind as he is eternally. But the truth is rather that God reveals himself to us in accordance with our capacity to understand him.

It is tempting to equate the three 'persons' of the Trinity with creation, salvation and sanctification, but this would be to attribute contrasting functions to each of the three persons and to treat them as separate, and Catholic tradition has refused to tread that path. Theologians have usually used two kinds of metaphor to clarify what is meant by saying that God is both three and one. There is the social analogy (such as that of two people and the love that unites them), and there is the psychological analogy (such as thinking, willing and feeling, each of these being separate activities which interpenetrate each other in a single person). Neither of these different approaches can provide more than remote analogies of the developed doctrine of interior relationships of the Holy Trinity. St Augustine wrote about this doctrine, as he put it, 'lest nothing be said'; but this did not prevent him writing thirteen books on the subject. I am suggesting that, however many books are written, nothing can be said.

Overdefinition in Doctrine

The doctrine was first formulated by the Church at the Council of Constantinople in AD 381, which confessed 'one and the same Godhead in the *hypostasis* of three Persons of equal honour and of equal power; namely Father, Son and the Holy Spirit'. According to the developed doctrine, the three persons 'coinhere', whatever may be the precise meaning of the phrase. The only distinction of the three lies in their origins. The Father is eternal, unbegotten and everlasting, the Son is eternally begotten and the Spirit proceeds from the Father and the Son (or, according to the original tradition which is still upheld by the Orthodox Churches, only from the Father). The 'procession' of the Spirit is so called from the use of that word in St John's Gospel, but there the reference is not to the eternal procession of the Spirit but rather to his coming into the world (John 15.26).

These are evidently metaphorical statements. At the same time it is not easy to understand what is the difference between eternal begetting and eternal procession. 'Begotten, not made' in the Nicene Creed is a phrase which is intended to put the Son beyond the sphere of creation: he is not an artefact. Eternal begetting is clearly metaphorical: taken literally, it is nonsensical. Begetting refers to a single personal act, procreation. If we are to distinguish between begetting and procession in a human person, we might say that the former refers to the sexual act whereby a man contributes part of himself to the formation of another person, whereas procession refers to an act of the autonomous system of the human body, such as emission of breath. (There is a sense in which breathing may be said to emit substance from a person, but it is a sub-personal activity.) The meaning of begetting and procession in relation to the Son and the Holy Spirit is unclear. Eternal begetting and eternal procession are even more difficult concepts, if indeed they can be said to be intelligible; and the idea of double procession (from the Father and the Son) is yet more difficult. But it is these distinctions, and these alone, that distinguish the Son from the

Holy Spirit, according to the orthodox doctrine of the Trinity. While 'the economic Trinity' is well grounded in Scripture as well as attested by Christian experience, 'the essential Trinity' is not directly revealed to us at all, but it is a development of the 'economic Trinity' of the Scriptures. It is not therefore to be denied, because it may be true, even if it is unintelligible. It lies beyond our human knowledge as well as our human understanding.

The greatest difficulty about the concept of the essential Trinity is the fact that we know nothing of the interior life of God. It is said that the Christian conviction that God's nature is pure love leads us towards the essential Trinity, since human love needs a subject to be loved, and the idea of a loving God existing in eternity without a person to love and to reciprocate that love is impossible to imagine. But the 'persons' of the Trinity are not persons in the sense in which we use the word today as subjects and objects of love, so what is true of human persons may not be true of God, for we know nothing of the inner life of God which is clothed and shrouded in mystery. We can only speak of his love in terms of metaphor from our knowledge of human love. God's eternal love cannot be imagined: we only know his love as he generously and freely bestows it upon us. Whenever we speak of God's nature (e.g. his justice, his mercy, his forgiveness) it can only be done by analogy from our knowledge of human beings. As the Eastern Orthodox put it, we can know the energies of God. But we do not know his essence. This apophatic view is well instanced in a well known and beloved hymn:

> Immortal, invisible, God only wise,
> In light inaccessible hid from our eyes,
> Most blessed, most glorious, the Ancient of Days,
> Almighty, victorious, thy great name we praise.

If God is so unknown, can we believe he is a personal God? Of course God is not a person such as we are, for human personality involves boundaries, and there are no boundaries in God. We can say that there is personality in God, and that not merely from experience. I find it impossible to believe that impersonal Reality would give rise to a creation in which human personality such as we know it has evolved. God must be suprapersonal to create such a universe. In any case he is not so utterly transcendent as the first verse of the hymn might suggest. The third verse begins:

> To all, life thou givest, to both great and small;
> In all life thou livest, the true life of all;

God is certainly transcendent; but it is a fact of our human experience that he is immanent as well: the technical word for this is panentheism.

Instead of starting from human experience, it is becoming popular to start theologizing from the unknown, from the dogma of the essential Trinity, and to argue theologically from this *a priori* startpoint. Trinitarian theology is said to be the basis of all true theology. It is spoken of as a revealed doctrine. It is nothing of the kind. It is an inference from the economic Trinity. Instead of the formula 'Glory to the Father and to the Son and to the Holy Spirit', could there not be an alternative formula, the more ancient formula of the Christian Church, according to which we come 'to the Father in the Spirit through Jesus Christ?'

The gains and losses of a more flexible approach, such as I have suggested in this chapter, need to be assessed. There are those who, believing that the Church has been guided by the Holy Spirit in these matters, prefer to keep the ancient traditions of the Church. Without the acceptance of Christ's two natures in one person they believe that the Christian faith loses its uniqueness and its salvific power, and that, without the notion of the exchange of love between the members of the Trinity, the Christian faith is eviscerated because, as they understand it, love always needs a subject. They hold that the essential Trinity is the proper startpoint for Christian theology.

On the other hand, those who prefer a more flexible approach find both the doctrine of two natures in one person intellectually unacceptable, and the developed doctrine of the Trinity unintelligible; and they believe that neither are really scriptural. They have a reverential agnosticism about the precise relationship of Christ to his Heavenly Father, and they insist on an apophatic approach to the internal life of God, about which we can know nothing whatsoever. They hold that it is more important to live as a disciple of Jesus than to hold a particular doctrine of his person, and more important to love God with heart and soul and mind than to hold an unintelligible doctrine of his inner nature. Further, they believe that a flexible approach would assist many lay people who have difficulty in assenting to what they cannot begin to understand. They also think that this would assist interfaith understanding, for members of other religions commonly believe that Christians are tritheists who believe in three Gods and idolaters who hold that Jesus is God. It must be emphasized that those in favour of a flexible approach are not withholding divinity from Christ or denying their trinitarian experience of God. They experience God through Christ and they strongly believe in the economic Trinity in the sense that God reveals himself to us in three modes as Father, Son and Holy Spirit, and that we approach God in the Spirit through Christ to the Father.

2

The Greatest Moral Challenge of All

The development of science and technology has produced fresh ethical questions that need to be addressed. Those most frequently in the news are concerned with sex, reproduction and death. I do not think that these are the most important questions. Nonetheless they do produce dilemmas for many people. With those cohabiting now at 17 per cent of the adult unmarried population, is the concept of marriage becoming outdated? If not, is all sexual intercourse outside marriage wrong? Is it right to use contraception? Are homosexual partnerships always wrong? If so, why did the Church bless them in the Middle Ages? Is *in vitro* fertilization wrong, when a husband's sperm is weak or feeble? Is it wrong to insert several foetuses in a womb in order to increase the chances of gestation, and then to remove some to prevent multiple births with little chance of survival? Is it ever morally right to use the 'morning after' pill? Is it right for a couple who cannot have children to use sperm donated by a third party, or a woman to have inserted in her womb some other woman's egg fertilized by her husband's sperm? Is all surrogate motherhood wrong? Is all cloning sinful? Is it wrong to use a foetus in its early stages for research into illnesses? May a 'cloned foetus' be used for this purpose? Is it wrong to use its stem cells to grow spare parts for human use? The list is long; but these are only some of the moral dilemmas over sex and reproduction most of which are posed by recent advances in medical science and technology, and which affect in a very intimate way the lives of many couples.

Again, there are questions concerning not the beginning of life but its end. Is it right to prolong existence on a life-support machine when there is no chance of recovery? Is it ever right to end life by withholding liquids when a person is mortally ill? Is it right to relieve pain by means of morphine when the result will be death? Is it ever right to assist suicide? The advances in medical technology have resulted in fresh dilemmas which have an added importance as people live to a greater and greater age. As the population ages, they will become more and more relevant. Indeed, one will soon have to ask whether it is right to prolong life by interfering with the ageing process.

These are important questions for individuals to solve, and I could wish that the non-Roman Churches produced more official guidance on these subjects to help people in their dilemmas. At the same time, they are not the most important moral questions which face humankind. Nor are issues concerning preparations for nuclear, chemical or biological warfare, whether as a result of an attack by terrorists or through confrontation between nations. These are very serious matters indeed, but not the most important.

The really urgent moral question confronting humankind concerns our present unsustainable use of non-renewable resources. When I first raised this question over thirty years ago (Montefiore, 1969) it seemed to many remote and academic: now it has become very relevant. We have been told that we do not own a freehold on our planet, but only a full repairing lease. That phrase was first used by Lady Thatcher when she was Prime Minister, and succeeding Premiers have spoken in favour of sustainable development. But no country and few individuals have yet taken the issue really seriously, at least so far as remedial action is concerned. There will have been a United Nations Summit at Johannesburg in the autumn of 2002 on the subject but, at the time of writing, preliminary indications suggest that little progress will have been made.

Sustainable development is surely the most important of all

questions. For the dilemmas concerning reproduction and death all presuppose that there is a future for civilized life on this planet. But the issue of sustainable development raises a question mark over the very future that awaits posterity. If it be agreed that it is necessary to reduce consumption of some natural resources from their present rates, this will involve changes of lifestyle for every individual, and it will also necessitate great changes in the laws of nations and in co-operation between nations. Sacrifices will be required that will be unpopular in an age of consumerism.

At first sight it might seem that the greatest problem is the ever increasing population of the world. It took until the early nineteenth century to reach a billion, another century to reach two billion, by the second half of the twentieth century to reach another billion, and now, at the beginning of the twenty-first century, it has already reached six billion, and it is still increasing, despite the tragic fact that (in addition to other killer diseases such as malaria and tuberculosis) a million people are dying every year of AIDS. The population of the world is still increasing, but no longer at an exponential rate. It is likely to peak by 2070 at nine billion (if all can be fed), and may fall to 8½ billion by 2100. It would level off more quickly if in the Third World more women could obtain education, if their standard of living increased and if contraception were available for all who want it. In a developed country such as the UK, population is actually projected to decrease by 2022.

It is rather ridiculous to ask whether there is enough food for the world's vast population, for the fact that people are alive shows there is at least a subsistence diet, even if millions exist at near-starvation level. Despite the fact that people in the developed world eat on average far more than they need (just as they consume far more raw materials than is their fair share) with the result that obesity is becoming common (one in three Americans and 16 per cent of our population in Britain), there would still be enough food for all if it were more equitably shared out. Nonetheless there is a limit to the amount of food that the earth can provide, just as there is a limit to the food that the oceans can provide, and that limit is fast being approached.

There are other problems which arise from an increasing world population. More and more non-renewable resources are consumed by more and more people. In the Third World more and more people are migrating towards the cities, which are overexpanding and which do not have the infrastructure to sustain such large numbers. Life in cities involves increased pressure and stress. In the animal world density regulation, and through this the control of numbers, is one of the main functions of their social organization. The stress of overcrowding causes aggression. It is the same with human beings. Intensity of conflict increases with population density.

The quest for more and more food naturally reduces the living space for wildlife. At the 'Cambrian explosion' 530 million years ago, large numbers of different multicellular life forms emerged, and since then some 30 million species have emerged. Species last between one and ten million years: the usual life span is four million. (*Homo sapiens,* if it behaves, has a long time still to go.) Today there are probably some 30 million different species, of which only 1,390,902 are known to us – the rain-forests contain (or used to contain) many more about which we know nothing. As circumstances change on earth, new forms of life become adapted to the new situation. Human beings now consume 40 per cent of the planet's primary productivity, which leaves comparatively little for other animals. In the past there have been five major extinctions (that is, periods when 65 per cent or more of all species disappeared). These were all due to natural causes, such as climate change or a meteor hitting the earth. We are today in the midst of the sixth extinction. It is made by us. It is of course never easy to be certain when a species is extinct, just as it is not easy to be certain how many species exist today on the earth and in the oceans. Numbers have certainly been exaggerated. But even conservative estimates put the rate at 1,500 times the natural rate of extinction (Lomborg, 2001, p. 255). The high extinction rate is caused by change of habitat (as we bring more land into cultivation), or by climate change, or by cutting down the rain-forests, or even by eating animal species to extinction as with some species of African monkeys. Extinctions have not merely been made of land-based animals: according to a recent survey, thousands of species of marine life have been extinguished, and others are endangered by deep-sea trawling. This raises a further moral question: have we the right to extinguish in this way whole species of animals, birds, insects (and fish too, by overfishing)? Most – but not all – people would agree that it is morally justifiable to kill animals for food or for medical purposes. But *whole species*? Those who believe that they exist under the providence of God are hard put to it to justify such slaughter.

As we have seen, the burgeoning population of the world is gradually being brought under control. It is not the main threat to the future of *Homo sapiens*. The real danger lies in the increasing pollution of the biosphere, and in the unsustainable use of land, forests, metals, minerals, water and fossil fuels.

Some of our problems are concerned with pollutants. Ozone in the upper atmosphere between 10 and 50 miles above the earth keeps out most of the dangerous cancer-causing ultraviolet rays of the sun. The 'ozone gap' is caused by the release of certain gases (such as those which used to be used in refrigerators) which ascend to the upper atmosphere and dissolve the ozone there. The gap is still found to be increasing, despite the Montreal Protocol agreed in 1987 in which 175 countries committed themselves to a tight schedule to phase out these ozone-depleting substances. Most of the countries are on target. The United Nations Environmental Fund formed a multinational fund eight years ago which has already paid out $1,000,000 towards enabling developing countries in the production of non-ozone depleting substances in accordance with the protocol. This is the one case where international co-operation has worked splendidly. Nonetheless it has been calculated that even if all such gases had been phased out by 1995, the ozone gap would still be with us into the twenty-second century. Already there has been a large increase in skin cancers due to the contraction of the ozone layer, and we have entailed this on future generations. The existence of a large brown cloud over South-East Asia, two miles high, is an augury of future trouble.

There are other forms of pollution with ill effects. The soil can be polluted by animal residues and the overuse of pesticides and fertilizer. The oceans are becoming polluted by plastics and other toxic stuffs which flow down rivers, and which cause damage to wildlife, including fish stocks. There is pollution of the air from nitrogen oxides (leading to human ailments) and acid rain has resulted in the loss of fish stocks, especially in Scandinavia. Water can suffer eutrophication and poisonous algae result from the run off of fertilizer residues. There are the 'gender bending' chemicals which can cause problems with reproductory systems (and which may be responsible for the apparent lowering of sperm count in men). Nobody yet knows the long-term effects of the genetic manipulation of agricultural produce. There is even fear of long-term effects from the use of mobile telephones and from radioactivity beneath pylons carrying the electricity grid. The dangers which can ensue when there is a fault in nuclear reactors are well known, and there is no known way of permanently storing radioactive residues. We live in an age of great technical advance, and we are glad to reap the short-term advantage of new technologies without knowing what their long-term consequences will be.

Apart from pollution there is the unsustainable use of raw materials (McLaren *et al.*, 1998, pp. 9ff.). One third of the planet consists of land which is crucial for tomorrow's world if people are to be fed. Crops need good soil, sufficient acreage, the right seeds, appropriate weather, and sufficient rain at the right time of the year. As mentioned above, soil can become polluted. World acreage of agricultural land is decreasing, despite 90 million more mouths to feed each year. Weather, as we have already noted, is becoming unsettled. Some of the best land is used for housing and road-building. Literally millions of acres of land are being turned into desert each year, partly due to bad irrigation which brings salts to the surface, and partly due to overgrazing by cattle, especially in those countries where wealth is counted in livestock.

The amount of livestock in the world is unsustainable. It has increased fourfold in 40 years. It seems hard to believe, but it is calculated that there are two billion four-legged livestock and 11 billion fowls in the world. They consume too much cereal food. Some countries cannot cope with all the slurry where there is intensive farming. Cattle produce methane gas from their residues and farts, a greenhouse gas which is twenty-five times worse than carbon dioxide: it accounts for 3 per cent of all greenhouse gases!

Forty million acres of forest have been cut down to provide for pastures for cattle in the last 20 years. Forests are vital for the welfare of the planet. They reverse the process of breathing, returning the carbon dioxide to the wood of the tree and sucking up large amounts of moisture from the soil and returning it to the atmosphere by evapotranspiration, whence it comes back as rain. It has been estimated that globally 20 per cent of the world's forests have been cut down since the dawn of agriculture. Some parts of the world have lost more than others; for example, Southern Asia and China have lost half of their forest cover in the last 300 years. Of particular concern are the tropical rain-forests, which have such a large effect on rainfall in those areas. They have been greatly plundered. During the 1980s 0.7 per cent of the total area of tropical rain-forests has been lost each year, although the latest study, based on satellite imagery, shows a fall in that amount. It is a wonderful natural ecosystem which humankind is destroying. Each year 37 million acres of forest is cut down for timber or for grazing land. When 70 per cent of a forest has gone, it cannot regenerate. Trees help to retain the topsoil, and prevent erosion. The role of ancient forests cannot be fully reproduced by new plantations.

The present use of wood is unsustainable. It is used for many many purposes, for which alternatives exist but are not used. Brushwood for heating and cooking – the only heating resource many in the Third World can afford – is becoming more and more difficult to find.

In addition to the prospect of flooding in the future, if the oceans rise as a result of the melting of polar ice, the world is running out of fresh water. Although irrigation, which up to 1978 was increasing at 3 per cent per annum, is no longer increasing at this rate, fresh water in some parts of the world is getting short because so much is still used for irrigation. In other regions, ground water is pumped from below the surface of the earth, which takes 750 years to replenish in the hydrological cycle. Rainfall is not distributed equally: there are parts of the world where very little falls. Much precipitation falls in remote areas where it cannot be utilized. Again, most rain falls at certain times of the year, and causes flooding; and this accounts for some three-quarters of the total rainfall. Some is conserved by dams, but the effect of water storage is ambiguous: the impoundment of three trillion tonnes of water in outsize dams has already pushed the axis of the earth's rotation away from the North Pole, and no one knows what the effects may be. Agriculture today accounts for over 70 per cent of global fresh water use, industry nearly a quarter and (on average) households 8 per cent. As the population increases, all these will require more water. Estimates of future water shortages vary greatly. Some predict that two-thirds of the world's population will be in water-stressed areas by 2025. Some three billion people will not have enough water to drink, to satisfy hygiene needs or to produce food, not to speak of the wider impact of water shortage on key ecosystems, such as forests and wetlands. Even by conservative estimates the proportion of water-stressed people will rise in the next half century to nearly one in five of the world's population. Clearly there needs to be better water allocation, less wasteful use and better water management. Of course much water is wasted, either in domestic use or through leakage. The world is running out of fresh water.

The main environmental challenge facing the world is global warming. Its main cause is the excessive use of fossil fuels. Some estimate that there is only another 50 years of oil that can economically be exploited at present rates of consumption, but in the past all such estimates have turned out to be gross underestimates. Clearly however we cannot expect to have oil reserves indefinitely; and so some substitute for the production of energy is required, and a substitute which does not involve the emission of carbon dioxide is urgently needed.

Again, the present use of many metals is unsustainable. For example, even conservative estimates reckon that there are reserves for only half a century or less of copper, gold, zinc, silver and tin at the present rates of consumption. The use of aggregates is such that it is interfering with environmental amenities. As for mining, not only does this involve the use of huge amounts of energy, but it also produces an enormous amount of waste (1 tonne of aluminium produces 50 tonnes of waste), and accounts for one quarter of the world's toxic wastes.

If our present development is unsustainable, what should be our strategy for the future? Since it will take some time to change present practices, it is best to consider what should be our goals 50 years ahead, in 2050. At the moment the developed world uses the overwhelming proportion of these resources. If a future strategy is to be based on the principles of natural justice, the future amount that each country should be able to use is the total sustainable resource of each category divided by the proportion of that country's population to world population in 2050. Without such distribution, the Third World will never be able to develop properly.

If we set our minds to it, this could be achieved. This is not the place to go into great detail, but to give a few examples, there are many substitutes for wood, such as plastics. Cattle require four pounds of cereal to produce one pound of meat. We should eat less meat, especially less beef. (The two worst enemies for the planet are cattle and the chainsaw.) In America, it is said, it takes two gallons of petrol to make a pound of pork. More organic farming would cut the use of fertilizers, which consume much energy in their manufacture. Instead of fossil fuels, there could be a large increase in renewable energy resources; there could be huge economies made by greater efficiency (for example, by combined heat and power schemes) and the use of less fertilizer which requires much energy to make; buildings could be constructed which have far better insulation and which need only a small proportion of present heating; motor cars could be 'hybrid'; and greater use could be made of hydrogen and the fuel cell, something that in any case will be necessary as oil reserves become scarce. So far as metals are concerned, there could be vastly more repair, re-use and reconditioning. (This would also save energy. A saucepan made from recycled aluminium uses only 5 per cent of the energy required if its metal is mined from bauxite.) An enormous amount of waste is recyclable, and this would save the need for landfill sites. The sums have been done, and if the UK set its mind to reduce its consumption of resources to the amount it would be allotted under the plan proposed above, it could be achieved without a reduction in our standard of living (McLaren *et al.*, 1998).

Global warming is the threat which currently engages most attention. The decade of the 1980s was the hottest for 1,000 years! It is well known that the so-called 'greenhouse gases' in the atmosphere allow the sun to irradiate the earth but do not allow its heat to escape back into outer space. Were it not for the existence of these gases, the mean temperature of the earth, it has been calculated, would be $-19°C$. So they can hardly be called pollutants! But greenhouse gases are building up faster than they can be buffered in the oceans or soaked up by green foliage. They are affecting the temperature of the planet and resulting in global warming. There are certainly a few anomalies that need clearing up, such as the curious fact that while the surface of the earth is warming up, the atmosphere above the earth seems unaffected. Nonetheless the 300 scientists who are involved in the International Panel on Climate Change (IPCC) warn that urgent action is needed to stabilize emissions of carbon dioxide and to curb the impact of these greenhouse gases on the climate of the planet. They hold that various factors, such as cleaner air, are causing the rate of warming to be double their previous forecasts, and they expect a rate of increase between $1.4°C$ and $5.8°C$ during the next century if nothing is done.

Ninety per cent of these greenhouse gases are emitted by the developed countries. A conference at Bonn in 2001 was held to finalize detailed rules for the implementation of an earlier treaty agreed at Kyoto in 1997 at which 178 nations agreed to reduce by 5.2 per cent levels of carbon dioxide emissions by 2010. The USA opted out of the agreement but 177 nations agreed on a target of 2 per cent reductions. The USA opted out for economic reasons, and has proposed voluntary targets which will only be met if they do not cut profits. Since then, Australia has refused to ratify. The treaty has been hailed as a great success, but in fact it was nothing of the kind. The USA produces a quarter of all such emissions, which will not be affected by the implementation of the treaty; and as now agreed the treaty has many exceptions, such as opting out of the requirement for reductions of carbon dioxide through planting new forests, or buying vouchers from other countries which have achieved more than their target, enabling the purchasing countries to exceed their emissions by that amount.

It is reckoned that the resulting reduction in temperature levels, provided that the target of 2 per cent reduction is achieved (and that is by no means certain), will be not more than 0.7°C! IPCC reckon that a climate increase of more than 0.1°C per decade is unacceptable, and to achieve an increase as low as this it will be necessary, by the end of the twenty-first century, to reduce current emissions of greenhouse gases from 22.2 gigatonnes a year to 2.2 gigatonnes, *a reduction of 90 per cent!* It is often said that the Bonn agreement is only a first step, but if there has been so much difficulty in reducing global warming by 0.7°C, how can agreement be found for a hugely larger reduction of 90 per cent? The amount that will be reduced under the agreement (if indeed all countries carry out their commitments) seems nugatory compared the vast reduction which is required by the end of the century. (Since the UK has only 1 per cent of the world's population, and emits 5 per cent of all greenhouse gases, its contribution should be correspondingly larger.)

What will be the result of increasing global warming? Oceans will rise, causing flooding, disastrous in the case of low-lying countries (and, incidentally, the Thames barrier). Weather will be unstable, producing droughts, fierce storms and unsettled conditions. Countries near the equator (where poverty is already very great) will be the worst affected. Patterns of agriculture will be disrupted. If the ice and snow in the polar regions melt, this will increase the pace of warming, as these reflect back the rays of the sun into the atmosphere. Diseases already common in the warmer parts of the earth will spread elsewhere. Ocean currents will alter. Here in the UK, although global warming presently results in more green foliage, and the swifts already stay here a week longer, things will change. In future it is likely to be much colder, as the fresh water from the melting polar ice will force the heavier salt water of the warm Gulf Stream underground, and the current will change direction, so that our climate is likely to be similar to that of Greenland.

The disruption will be very great. No doubt *Homo sapiens* will adjust, but as a result of all this upheaval, millions are likely to die.

This is causing me to have second thoughts about nuclear energy, a distressing situation for one who has been chairman of the Trust of Friends of the Earth which has campaigned (and still does) so doughtily against nuclear energy, with which I have until lately agreed. It is the urgency of the present situation that is causing me a change of heart. Our government has targets to increase energy efficiency by 20 per cent, and to increase renewable sources for electricity by the same amount, by 2020. But targets are seldom met, and it is hard to see how further economies can be made after that. Attempts to reduce carbon dioxide emissions by 90 per cent by the end of this century will never be successful under an energy economy dominated by fossil fuels. Although there are real advances in energy from renewable resources these are not yet economical contrasted with fossil fuels. Energy from these sources is unlikely to be available in sufficient amounts and at economic prices soon enough to avoid calamity. Yet a 90 per cent reduction in carbon dioxide is needed by 2099 to safeguard the future of the planet against disastrous climate change. It is just conceivable that without nuclear energy it could be made to happen, if everyone and all nations were to co-operate. But they don't and they won't. Stringent economies would have to be introduced, far greater energy efficiencies implemented, vastly greater energy from renewable sources would have to be available. This would require a radical change of heart among the developed nations. Certainly there has been, in the last half century, a remarkable acceptance of environmentalism as an idea to be embraced, but not as a basis for action to be taken. We live in a materialist culture, and people are unwilling to curtail the profligate use of energy which is part of their way of life.

Already renewable resources of energy such as photovoltaics, fuel cells, wind power, wave power and geothermal energy (in place of fossil fuels) are being exploited to a small degree. Apart from wind power they are not yet economic (and we cannot have our beautiful countryside ruined by wind machines), and they are most unlikely to be available in sufficient quantities in time to be substituted for our present use of fossil fuels, until it is too late. These substitutes will not be available in time to prevent a grave increase in global warming. Those who think that the danger of future global warming can be averted by the combination of a technological fix and a willingness by people in a materialist culture to alter their lifestyle in order to prevent future calamity are living in cloud cuckoo land. A technological fix is most improbable. Liberal humanism is incurably optimistic, but a more realistic Christian view acknowledges that human nature is deeply flawed, as indicated by our present self-indulgent materialist culture.

Should we then resign ourselves to a calamitous situation of a warmer planet with a higher sea level, resulting in the probable death of millions and in grave disruption to civilized life as we know it? I do not think so. There is an alternative – nuclear energy, which is produced without the emission of greenhouse gases. (Certainly this will not solve all our energy problems. Nuclear energy, and non-renewable sources of energy (including the fuel cell which is, however, very unlikely to become economic in the near future) do produce electricity; but motor vehicles can only run a comparatively short distance on an electric battery before recharging, and people will not give up the use of the motor car.)

Twenty per cent of our energy in the UK is now being produced by nuclear power. But our Magnox Reactors are reaching the end of their life. There are, I know, strong arguments against building more reactors. Reactors are expensive to build and to run they would probably need government subsidies; but wind machines already receive subsidies. Large nuclear reactors need to be protected against terrorism, but so do other installations. We ourselves have had in the UK a major accident in 1957 at what is now called Sellafield, and as a result people have died – the only son of a farmer whose family lived close to our holiday house in the hills of Wales, where the pollution was heaviest, died of leukaemia. Then there was trouble at Three Mile Island in 1979, and the appalling tragedy of Chernobyl in 1986. Nuclear energy scares people, in the same way that nuclear bombs are so frightening, because the danger is invisible. Since Three Mile Island no more reactors have been built in the UK.

But these accidents, ghastly as they were, need to be set beside over 800 nuclear power stations active in the world today. If properly built, managed and protected, nuclear reactors are perfectly safe. In the last 50 years Japan, which has no other indigenous source of energy, has built 49 reactors, without an incident. Most of these power plants are performing well. New ideas are in the air, and the favourite is the pebble-bed hopper, a design that should be cheap, safe and efficient. The density of uranium in the reactor is not sufficient to start a runaway meltdown. As the fuel comes in small ceramic-wrapped pebbles, it is easier to handle than control rods. It is unlikely, however, that many sites could be found away from human habitations suitable for large-scale reactors, so there is interest in another kind of reactor which is being developed in Japan, a 200 kilowatt reactor only 6 metres high and 2 metres wide which could fit into the basement of an office block (Hadfield, 2001, pp. 3–4). Undoubtedly there will be questions that must rightly be asked about cost and safety in any new type of reactor, and risk of contamination by long-term highly radioactive nuclear residues must be assessed. A fundamental objection to nuclear energy is that there is no agreed method of storing high-level radiation wastes, so we might be accused of leaving our dangerous rubbish to posterity to cope with. If the world shifts to nuclear energy, there is likely, sooner or later, somewhere or other, to be some kind of terrible accident. The fundamental question, however, is this: which is worse, some loss of life in a possible nuclear accident or the near certainty of major disruption and loss of life through the effects of global warming?

The question, as I see it, is whether the dangers to posterity from the effects of energy from nuclear fuel are greater than the dangers to posterity from the effects of global warming. I think not.

Whatever course is taken over the source of future supplies of energy, there still remain the problems caused by pollution and the overexploitation of the non-renewable resources of the planet. The result is the upsetting of ecosystems which have naturally evolved, and the disruption of their feedback mechanisms which keep the planet comfortable for life. 'Gaia must be seen as a single physiological system, an entity which is alive at least to the extent that, like other living organisms, its chemistry and temperature are self-regulated at a state comfortable for life' (Lovelock, 1979, p. 11). We are interfering with the stability of the planet, which will produce ill effects for the future of humankind.

Even if there does occur an environmental disaster (whether from nuclear power or lack of renewable resources or from global warming and pollution), good could result from this evil. Planet Earth and its ambient atmosphere have evolved, by divine providence, in such a way that its self-assembling mechanisms maintain and make it comfortable for life. If humankind continues to act so foolishly as seriously to threaten these systems, it is likely that humankind will, by natural causes, be eliminated. However, if it is part of God's will that humankind should survive, it may be that by divine providence humankind brings upon itself an environmental calamity of such a kind that it makes people change their ways. I have long thought that things are likely to get worse before they get better, and that an environmental calamity is needed to frighten people into avoiding a global catastrophe. People are so wedded to their consumerist and materialist way of life that duty and explanation, exhortation and encouragement are not enough. They will only change their lifestyles when to these are added fear.

If the world is to change from overexploitation to sustainable development, great changes will be needed, both in personal life-styles and in national strategies. For example, we shall have to rely on public transport more and the private motor car less. We shall have to change not only the way in which we use energy to fulfil our needs, but also the kind of energy that we use. It is imperative that changes should take place as soon as possible. Government policies must reflect such changes. The tax system will have to be changed so that the tax on goods reflects the amount of energy used in their manufacture. (This applies to services as well as goods: air travel is cheap at the moment because there is no tax on aviation fuel.) Goods will have to be produced which are meant to last and do not have built-in obsolescence. Many of these changes will be unpopular: nevertheless they will have to take place, if the world is to be made safe for posterity.

Not only will there have to be changes in personal lifestyles and government policies: there will also have to be international agreements. For example, if one country introduces a tax on aviation fuel, and another does not, the former will be at an economic disadvantage, and will lose either profit on a journey or (if it raises prices) customers. Will the Third World co-operate in changes such as stopping the destruction of rain-forests, realizing that most of the damage has been and is being done for consumption in the developed world (which, in Europe at least, cut down its own forests in earlier ages)? Will the developed countries be willing to compensate them for this? Will they be prepared to put the wellbeing of the planet in front of their own economic success? At the moment, the USA, the richest country in the world and its greatest carbon pollutant, puts the economy in front of ecology.

This is the greatest moral challenge facing human beings. They live on a planet surrounding a middle-aged, middle-sized star in a universe which began from an infinitesimal speck at the Big Bang some 13 billion years ago. The universe has expanded since then to an unimaginably vast size. Astronomers have a horizon of ten billion light years, that is to say, the distance that light can travel in ten billion years. That is as far as we can get: no one knows the universe's ultimate extent or even whether it is part of a great multiverse. Within the immensity of the universe there is mostly empty (or nearly empty) space; but there are also literally billions of galaxies, and more in the process of formation; and our star, the Sun, is only one of billions of stars in our own galaxy, the Milky Way. Whether or not there are other planets circling other stars in the universe where life has developed we do not know, but there are good reasons for thinking that this may not be so. They could not have developed long before ours, because all the elements on our planet (and in our bodies) are derived, as they would be on another planet, from the explosions of an earlier generation of stars. It seems that God thought good to create all this apparent waste and excess because he wanted intelligent life to develop capable of making free choices: it is hard to imagine any other reason. Perhaps life on this earth is absolutely unique. Our sun has run nearly half its life: it has another 5 billion years ahead of it. Barring impacts from meteorites, our Planet Earth has a long life ahead. And yet we are endangering posterity on earth through thoughtlessness and greed. It is in this context that sustainable development faces human beings with their greatest moral challenge.

Sustainable development poses three sets of questions. First, can people be made to realize the urgency of this present crisis? At the moment few are aware of the challenge. Second, will individuals be prepared to co-operate in making the necessary changes of lifestyle, even if some of these interfere with their convenience? At the moment in the developed world at least, there is an avid consumerism, a greed for possessions, encouraged by advertising, which makes such changes in lifestyle seem improbable. Third, will the nations not only agree to make the necessary changes, but actually keep their agreements, and penalize those who do not keep to agreed targets? These are the greatest questions facing humankind.

3

Jewish Christians

Most Christians assume that all other Christians, like themselves, are not Jewish.

For most of the two thousand years of its existence the Christian Church has been almost entirely Gentile, that is to say, it has consisted of non-Jews. Originally, of course, the Church was entirely Jewish. Jesus in his earthly ministry ministered almost entirely to Jews ('I am not sent but unto the lost sheep of the house of Israel' (Matthew 15.24 (AV); cf. 10.6), even if, according to the Gospels, he never turned away Gentiles on the few occasions when they came to him. The twelve Apostles of course were all Jews, so were the 3,000 said in the Acts to have been baptized on the first Christian Pentecost (Acts 2.42); so much so that they 'continued daily with one accord in the Temple'. It was not until later that the first Gentiles were baptized in Caesarea, and that only because, as Peter recounted to the Jerusalem Church, they had received the Holy Spirit like the earliest (Jewish) believers.

Jewish Christians had earlier suffered persecution in Judaea and, as a result, they had been scattered abroad in the Jewish dispersion in the Mediterranean region, where inevitably they mingled with Gentiles as well as Jewish Christians. Equally inevitably, Gentiles were converted. According to Acts 15 a council was called in Jerusalem to regulate the entry of Gentiles into the Church. The Apostle Paul regarded it as his vocation to be the apostle to the Gentiles, for which he managed to gain approval from the 'pillars' of the Church at Jerusalem. His decision that Gentiles need not keep the Jewish law and that

Gentile males need not be circumcised before their admission to the Church provoked controversy among Jewish Christians. Though the majority of Christians were still Jews, the Church now consisted of both Jews and Gentiles.

At that stage the centre of the Church was in Jerusalem, but the situation changed after the fall of the city to the Romans in AD 70, and the main centres of the Church became located in the large coastal towns of the Mediterranean. There were of course Jewish Christians, with a wide spectrum of belief, ranging from strict observance of the Jewish law to a more liberal outlook, and from regarding Jesus as a prophet to worshipping him as Son of God (Dunn, 1972, p. 262). But the Gentiles began to predominate in the Church. The gulf between Judaism and Christianity widened, so that the Christian Church was no longer a sect within Judaism (which was how it began) but became a rival religion. There were still Jewish Christians in Judaea, known as Ebionites, although they did not long continue and little for certain is known about them: we only have negative remarks from the early Church Fathers. But early Jewish practices died hard over matters such as fast days and the Jewish sabbath; and there was a protracted debate over the date of Easter, which those who wished to keep it according to the Jewish Passover tradition eventually lost. However, Judaism, with its customs and its Scriptures in the original Hebrew, still had a certain attraction for Christians in the early Church, at any rate in Constantinople. We know this through a series of vitriolic sermons preached by its Archbishop, John Chrysostom, against the Jews, the object of which was to prevent Christians from attending synagogue worship. Christians with a Jewish origin were pressurized to conform to the practices of Christianity without a backward glance at the religion from which they had originally sprung (and from which Christianity itself had grown).

In a largely Gentile Church, negative attitudes towards Jewish belief and practice naturally rubbed off on Jewish Christians.

The third-century *Didascalia Apostolorum* warned against Jewish customs. The *Apostolic Constitutions* forbade Christians to enter synagogues. The Council of Laodicea pronounced that it was not lawful to receive unleavened bread from Jews or to be partakers of their 'impiety'. A later profession of faith from Constantinople made a person say: 'I renounce all customs, rites, legalisms, unleavened breads and sacrifices of the Hebrews... I renounce absolutely everything Jewish, every law, rite and custom...'. Even as late as AD 787 the Second Council of Nicaea denounced those who 'secretly keep the Sabbath and observe other Jewish customs'. Jewish Christianity had been proscribed. Of course there were Christians who came from the Jewish tradition. But they kept very quiet about their origins, and conformed to the traditions of a now overwhelmingly Gentile Church. It was a complete turnaround from the situation in which the Church began.

Thus the situation continued throughout the Middle Ages and beyond. The worst medieval persecution took place in Central Europe in 1348–50 (Küng, 1992, p. 170). Sporadic persecution does not seem to have resulted in many Jews joining the Church, but there were of course occasional Jewish converts. They were required to give up their Judaism, and if possible, the Church tried to use them to oppose their former co-religionists. From time to time enforced baptism of Jews took place. For example, in 1391 there were 12,000 forced baptisms in Valencia in Spain. In that country Jews had reached high positions in the state, but in 1492 Ferdinand and Isabella confronted them with a choice: either to be expelled or to be baptized. Many left the country, but others were baptized. Most of these secretly kept up Jewish customs. They were known as *Marranos* (pigs). The Inquisition busied itself trying to root them out. Even St Teresa of Avila, because of her Jewish blood, at one time fell under suspicion. Although these Jewish Christians could not openly practise their Judaism or allow it to influence their Christian worship, they must have considerably increased the number of Jewish Christians within the Church.

The position began to change with the Enlightenment. A few Jews converted to Christianity because of financial gains for so doing, especially in Prussia. Later in Germany many Jewish families became 'integrated ' because it was the first step on the ladder towards a career in a university or the armed forces. There was quite a lot of intermarriage between Jews and Christians, both in England and the continent of Europe. Later on, under the Nazis, Jews in Germany did not escape persecution through conversion, but the Nazis, to their surprise, found many of their citizens had half or a quarter Jewish blood.

At the beginning of the nineteenth century the first English mission to Jews was formed, and a number of distinguished Jewish figures were drawn to Christianity (Cohn-Sherbok, 1992, p. 15). The Christian mission to Jews spread to Eastern Europe and America. Quite apart from these agencies, there were genuine conversions, and these have continued to this day. In 1845 Michael Alexander, who was a Jewish-Christian Anglican priest, was consecrated bishop in Jerusalem; but the appointment was a disaster, and he died not long after going to Palestine. In 1866 the Hebrew Christian Alliance was formed in England, and a similar branch in the USA in 1915; and in 1925 the Alliance became internationalized. It still continues today, and I used to belong to it, but I resigned when it changed its name to an Alliance of Messianic Jews because of my unwillingness to be counted among them.

On the continent of Europe in the nineteenth century there were several prominent Jews who became 'Jewish believers', who believed in Christ but kept to a Jewish way of life, such as Rabbi Abraham Schwarzenberg of Poland, Theodor Lucky of Galicia and Rabbi Lichtenstein of Hungary. These did not attempt to form a Jewish-Christian Church. But Joseph Rabinowitsch did. He called his Jewish-Christian community in Bessarabia

'Israelites of the New Covenant'. Then Paul Levertoff of Russia came to believe that Christianity fulfils the hopes of Judaism, and had great influence in Eastern Europe. Sacked from his chair in Rabbinics in Leipzig, he came to England in 1919, was priested in the Church of England and appointed to the parish of Holy Trinity, Shoreditch, where he tried to form a Jewish-Christian Church within the 'Church Catholic'. But all these movements petered out after the death of their leaders.

In 1942 there was formed in the UK the Council for Christians and Jews. Its chief aim was to combat anti-Semitism, in view of the Nazi persecution of Jews; and as such it did excellent work. But it has not done serious work on the relationship of Judaism and Christianity. My relations with it have not been happy. One of my two brothers (both practising Jews) used to work for it in a voluntary capacity. When hoping to do likewise I later approached William Simpson, its genial secretary, who advised me to keep out, as the presence of a Jewish Christian would not be appreciated. Some twenty years ago I sent for publication in the Council's magazine a lecture I had given in a Liberal Jewish synagogue on the convergence of Jewish and Christian ethics. Accepted by its (Christian) editor it was later rejected by its (Jewish) Director. I have come to regard its name as somewhat of a misnomer: it seems to me – I hope wrongly – a Council of Jews and Gentile Christians.

In the middle of the twentieth century, there emerged a movement of so-called Messianic Jews. These people assert their Judaism and keep as much as possible to Jewish traditions but believe fervently in Jesus as Messiah. Nonetheless its adherents seem to me to put their Jewishness in front of their Christianity. The movement has grown particularly in the USA: there, out of 6,000,000 Jews it is alleged that 300,000 have joined the 100 or so Messianic Jewish congregations. These function somewhat like independent Baptist chapels. They practise baptism, but do not use the word, because of its sinister echoes for Jews of forcible baptisms in earlier days: they prefer the word *mikveh*, the Jewish word for a ritual bath. The movement which calls itself 'Jews for Jesus' has gained a notorious reputation among orthodox Jews for unfair methods of proselytism.

There are a few communities of Messianic Jews in the UK (Fieldsend, 1993). In Israel there are some 40 congregations, which are frowned upon by orthodox Jews, but permitted to exist in a country which allows freedom of worship. Jewish-Christian congregations allow Gentile Christians to join them, and claim that some have done so. Messianic Judaism is an indigenous movement in the sense that it was started by Jews, who form the overwhelming majority of members, and it has nothing to do with Gentile Christian evangelism.

Jewish Christianity must be seen in relation to Christianity's attitude to Judaism. 'Supersessionism' is the belief that Christianity has superseded Judaism, which has forfeited the promises of God. This was, until the middle of the twentieth century, the general Christian view. It followed that, as Christians saw it, Jews were as much in need of Christian mission as any adherent of a heathen religion; in fact, more so, since Jesus had originally brought the good news to Jews. Such a view reinforced the anti-Semitism which had been endemic in the Christian Church for nearly two thousand years, and which had resulted in gross violation of their human rights, without which the Holocaust could never have taken place. However, after the Holocaust's horrors became generally known, there took place among Christians a radical reappraisal to which James Parkes had already led the way (Parkes, 1934). Judaism is now seen by most Christians as a religion in its own right. Because God's gifts and call are irrevocable (Romans 11.29), it is generally accepted by Christian theologians that God's Covenant with the Jews still holds, and has not been superseded by the New Covenant in Jesus Christ.

For very good reasons, then, attention has focused on

Christians' attitude towards Jews, and on a positive evaluation of the Jewish faith; but as a result, the position of Jewish Christians has been almost entirely overlooked. An attempt was made to bring up the relationship of church and synagogue at the Lambeth Conference in 1988. I caught sight of the draft document which said, *inter alia*, that Christians should read the New Testament and Jews should read the Talmud (or words to that effect). Had this draft been passed, I would have felt forced to leave the Church of England, for although Jewish I intend to go on reading and being nourished by the New Testament. Fortunately there was an outcry, and the draft was not published. Instead there was substituted in the Conference Report an appendix on 'Jews, Christians and Muslims: The Way of Dialogue'. The dialogue, such as it is, has been taken up by the Churches' Commission on Interfaith Relations, which published a report in 1994 called *Christians and Jews: A New Way of Thinking*.

More lately, the Church of England has taken some action of its own. In 2001 it appointed an officer whose duty is to advise on the issues which the Holocaust raises for the Church of England. When questioned about the implications of the Holocaust for Christian mission to the Jews, the officer replied that it was her personal opinion that mission to the Jewish people was inappropriate. I think she would have been wise to explain what she meant by mission. If aggressive evangelism or proselytism or manipulative pressure was intended, then she was right: it is inappropriate towards anyone, Jews or non-Jews. It would be an attack on people's integrity. Because of the special circumstances of Jewish–Christian relations over the centuries, in which anti-Semitism has been rife and coercion has been practised, the idea of Christians as the enemies of Jews has sunk deep into the Jewish subconscious, and it has become part of their folk religion, so that any attempt at evangelism of any kind is, in my judgement, not only inappropriate but also counterproductive.

But there is a wider sense of the word 'mission', a word which primarily means 'being sent' and which derives for Christians from their conviction that Christ was sent into the world for wholeness and salvation. It involves being as well as doing. The very presence of Christian men and women, living the Christian life and showing unconditional loving-kindness to other men and women is itself a form of mission. It is an essential aspect of Christian mission to show disinterested love to others, and in the light of the terrible past history of Christian anti-Judaism, Christians need to show this particularly to Jewish people. Mission also includes all forms of Christian service, both personal service given by individuals to other people, and also action at a corporate level to serve groups of people in need. In this sense mission is not only wholly appropriate: indeed it is an integral part of the gospel.

To return to the Church of England, in 1996 in the General Synod a question was asked by the late Michael Vasey, a respected evangelical:

> In view of the recent statements issuing from the Council of Christians and Jews, what plans does the Board have to express the Church of England's support for those of its members who see themselves as both Jewish and Christian, and to affirm their active involvement in sharing the Good News of the Messiah with their fellow Jews?

There ensued a certain amount of buck-passing among the committees and subcommittees of the Archbishops' Council. Questions of support were to be referred to the Committee for Minority Ethnic Anglican Concerns (which has kept a discreet silence on the matter). Questions of mission to those of other faiths go to the Inter-Faith Consultancy Group (IFCG), which has produced a Report on Jewish–Christian relationships. This was shown to the House of Bishops, and alterations were made as a result of their comments, although its authority is only that of the Group that owned it. *Sharing One Hope?* (ed. Ipgrave, 2001) is subtitled *Christian–Jewish relations*, which well describes its contents. (It is curious that nowhere in the Report is the New Covenant which Jesus initiated mentioned in this connection.)

So Michael Vasey's question remains unanswered.

The Report does however devote a chapter two pages long to people who are described rather strangely as 'Jewish people who believe in Jesus'. (Would non-Jewish Christians like to be described as 'Gentile people who believe in Jesus'?) This chapter is all but entirely taken up by a discussion of Messianic Jews (and a later appendix contains some very searching questions that should be put to them). Jewish members of the mainstream Churches receive the barest mention, in one sentence of the chapter, as though they hardly exist. They do of course far outnumber the number of Messianic Jews in the UK. The Report does once mention the dividing wall of hostility between Jews and Gentiles which, according to Ephesians 2.14–16, Christ has broken down. It asks Messianic Jews whether this accords with their practice. Significantly, no such question is put to the Christian Church.

Since there is no light from this Report about an answer to Michael Vasey's question, I shall take it upon myself to attempt an answer.

So far as mission to the Jews is concerned, it is wrong, in my judgement, to engage in evangelism towards them; and there is a sense in which it is not strictly necessary, since they worship the one true God and, if they keep to the demands of the Covenant which God made with them, they have been promised salvation. The Roman Catholic Church has no organization set up for the conversion of Jews (Fisher, 2001, p. 1013). But what happens if a Jew asks a Christian about the Christian faith? It is surely appropriate for Christians to tell individual Jews, if they are asked, what the Christian faith means to them, and how it affects their life. If Jews want to go further, and wish to join the

Christian Church, they should be invited to go back to the Jewish faith in which God had placed them by birth, and only to depart from it if it is found lacking in some essential or if it can no longer be practised with integrity. At that stage it would be appropriate to agree to instruction for Christian baptism.

What then should be the attitude of Gentile Christians towards such a convert from Judaism? Perhaps convert is not the *mot juste*, because Jews who become Christians do not leave behind their Jewish heritage so much as find it fulfilled in Christianity. Should such a Jewish Christian be welcomed? St Paul was in no doubt that a warm welcome should be given. We need not concern ourselves with the identity of the author of the Epistle to the Ephesians, whether it was actually by the hand of St Paul or written, as some think, by a Paulinist in line with his thinking. In it we find the following written to 'the Gentiles in the flesh':

> But now in Christ Jesus you who once were far off have been brought near in the blood of Christ. For he is our peace, who has made us both one, and has broken down the dividing wall of hostility... that he might create in himself one new man in place of two, so making peace... (Ephesians 2.15)

I fear that the dividing wall is still there, not only with Messianic Jews but also in most of the mainstream Churches. For Jewish Christians do not receive a special welcome into the Church. Rather like the early Jewish Christians in Jerusalem when they heard of the baptism of the Gentile Cornelius, Gentile Christians concur but do not usually rejoice at the prospect of having a Jewish Christian in their midst.

Christians have at last validated the Jewish religion, and that is right and proper. But in their keenness to affirm Jews and to avoid giving them any offence, they tend to avoid all mention of Jewish Christians, as though they wish that they would go away, fearing that they may muddy the waters of their new *rapprochement* with the Jewish people. While I am delighted at this new relationship between Christians and Jews, could it be the case that, just as the Macpherson Report suggested that there is institutionalized racism in the police force, so also a kind of institutionalized racism exists *inside* the Christian Church? Nothing overt, of course, but Jewish Christians (considered apostates by Orthodox Jewry) are usually regarded as a quaint ethnic minority oddity, whereas, according to St Paul, they form a vital constituent of the Church. It is no surprise to find that a Report, supposedly produced in answer to a question about Jewish Christians, has been written entirely by Gentile Christians.

Yet for St Paul the Church was not complete without the inclusion of both Jews and Gentiles. In the Epistle to the Ephesians he speaks of Gentiles as fellow heirs with Jews; and he writes of his own vocation to preach to Gentiles the unsearchable riches of Christ and to make known this divine plan of the mystery that has previously been hidden. And what is this previously hidden mystery? It is that Jews and Gentiles are members of the one body and partakers together of the promises of Christ through the gospel (Ephesians 3.1–9). While Paul in his day had to make it known to Jewish Christians that they were fellow heirs with Gentile Christians, it seems that, vice versa, the reverse is true today. When I pointed out that in *Sharing One Hope?* the need for the Church to contain both Gentile and Jewish Christians is not mentioned, and that without this the Church is deficient, the reply was given that this was the premise from which the working group which produced the Report began. If only this were really the case!

Jewish Christians have been given gifts by God to contribute to the Church of God. They have been accustomed in Judaism to liturgies which are full of thanksgiving, something that certainly cannot be said of Cranmer's Prayer Book, and only marginally so of the subsequent *Alternative Service Book* and

Common Worship. Again, as members of the Jewish community they will have attended weddings where the liturgy is full of joy and gladness (as instanced in the Seven Blessings of the Bride and Bridegroom), a contrast to Christian marriage liturgies. They have come from a strong tradition of Jewish family solidarity and Jewish family worship, in which the father of the family acts, as it were, as the priest of the family. These are just some of the gifts which Jewish Christians can contribute to the richness of the Church.

While the Churches must continue to reach out in love and friendship to members of the Jewish faith, they should also be prepared to show that catholicity requires the presence of both Gentiles and Jews within the Church.

4

Ecumenism, not Reunion

I was in my first year at theological college, and the World
Council of Churches was about to come into being in the early
autumn of 1948. We were all very excited. A decisive step forward
towards the reunion of Christendom seemed about to take place.
I remember going to Woudschoten in Holland for a student
conference in connection with the inauguration of the WCC in
Amsterdam. We were visited by the bigwigs from the conference.
We sang together in unison well known hymns translated into
different languages: this seemed like a symbol of what we hoped
would shortly come to pass. It still remains vivid in my memory,
although it took place over half a century ago. I can remember
the sessions (and also the novelty of cheese served at breakfast. It
was shortly after the War, and we had not the experience of
today's modern travel).

Was our enthusiasm misplaced? Today the WCC has been
largely marginalized. Nobody – and no Church – takes much
notice of it, although literally hundreds of Churches belong to it.
It publishes books, reserved mainly for its own faithful followers.
It has recently eschewed large conferences. Undoubtedly it does
good work, but often in little known and unpublicized ways, such
as dialogues with other faiths. It is said that the Orthodox
Churches are thinking of withdrawing, because they do not feel
that they receive fair treatment among so many Protestant
Churches. The Roman Catholic Church has never joined – how
could it, since it holds that the Church subsists in their Church,
and that (apart from the Orthodox Churches which retain what
it counts as the apostolic succession and a valid Eucharist) all the

other Churches are not even 'proper Churches'? Nonetheless, the Roman Catholic Church does co-operate with the WCC in matters of faith and order.

It might seem that the WCC is going the way of the old League of Nations, to which many nations belonged but which few if any took seriously. But it might be that, while the WCC as an institution has passed its prime, the basis of its existence, the unity of the Christian Church, is now high on the agenda of Churches, so that the Council is scarcely needed. It might even be that the WCC, by reason of its size and bureaucracy, with its headquarters at Geneva, has become a kind of ecumenical denomination of its own.

In one sense the notion of Christian unity has made immense strides in the last 50 years. Whereas ministers of different denominations then might well have avoided meeting one another in the street and having to engage in the civilities of intercourse, now they are often firm friends, and instead of regarding one another as rivals and even as enemies, they now acknowledge one another as allies and fellow-workers in the service of Christ. That is a colossal gain. Furthermore, friendships have grown up between the lay members of different Churches. The whole ecumenical atmosphere has radically altered. Archbishop William Temple, even before the second Great War had ended, had called ecumenism 'the great new fact of our era'.

Another immense gain is the ecumenical stance of the Roman Catholic Church since the Second Vatican Council. Earlier, that Church, by far the largest in all Christendom, had only one view of ecumenism, and that was the return of all other Churches to the Roman Catholic Church. I can remember the time when Roman Catholics were not even permitted to say the Lord's Prayer with other Christians! At the Second Vatican Council (1963–5) there was a radical change. There could even be joint services. 'Although the ecumenical movement and the desire for reconciliation with the Catholic Church has not yet grown universally strong, it is our hope that the ecumenical spirit and mutual esteem will gradually increase among all men' (*Unitatis Redintegratio*, 19). More lately, Pope John Paul II has repeatedly said that the Roman Catholic Church is irrevocably committed to ecumenism, and to this end it has been engaged in conversations with representatives of various non-Roman Churches. Roman Catholics are members of local Councils of Churches in the UK. In Birmingham, for example, the Roman Catholic Archbishop, the Church of England bishop and the Methodist Chairman of District are all ex officio Presidents of the Birmingham Council of Christian Churches, and non-eucharistic joint services of worship are held regularly under its auspices.

It was not long after the inauguration of the WCC that difficulties concerning reunion came to light in the Church of England with the proposed formation of the Church of South India, which included both Anglican priests and ministers from non-episcopal Churches (but which only united a minority of Christians in the area). The new Church would be fully episcopal, but those ministers of the non-episcopal Churches which would merge into the new Church would not be required to have a formal episcopal ordination, but would count as fully validated presbyters of the new Church (which was in fact inaugurated in September 1947). The Church of England had to decide whether Anglican priests who joined the new Church were to be regarded as schismatics or welcomed back as priests if they paid a return visit to England. The Church found itself engaged in sometimes acrimonious debate, which hinged on the nature of episcopacy, whether it should be regarded as of the 'esse', 'plene esse' or merely the 'bene esse' of the Church. It was decided that episcopally-ordained ministers of the South Indian Church should be welcomed at Anglican altars, but that non-episcopally-ordained clergy should not. Eventually the latter retired or died out, as all new ordinations in the South Indian Church were carried out by regularly-ordained bishops. If the Church was so divided about its relationships with a far-off church, what chance was there of reunion nearer home?

The answer to that question would shortly be decided. Archbishop Fisher in 1946 had preached a University Sermon at Great St Mary's, Cambridge, in which he felt the time had not yet come for reunion but invited the Free Churches to 'take episcopacy into their system'. The Methodist Church took up this suggestion and a reconciliation of the two Churches was proposed. There ensued protracted negotiations and reports on Anglican and Methodist reunion. Archbishop Fisher, who by this time had retired, opposed the scheme because he did not want a merger, but it was backed by his successor, Archbishop Michael Ramsey. The crux was the reconciliation of Anglican and Methodist ministries. A form of words made it ambiguous whether Methodist ministers were being reconciled with the laying on of hands, or whether they were being episcopally ordained. Anglo-Catholics, who did not mind receiving Holy Communion at the same altar with fellow Anglicans despite the fact that they understood the Eucharist differently from themselves, nevertheless felt in conscience bound to reject ambiguity in the proposed Service of Reconciliation. The scheme had passed all the hurdles but this. It was agreed by the Methodist Conference, but it was finally rejected a very late stage by the Church of England's General Synod in 1972: it was like jilting the bride at the altar as wedding vows were about to be taken.

Archbishop Fisher's Cambridge sermon provoked an initiative with the Church of Scotland. *The Bishops' Report* in 1957 proposed that bishops, consecrated by Anglicans, were to be appointed as permanent Moderators of presbyteries in England and Scotland. It got nowhere. It was decisively rejected by the General Assembly of the Church of Scotland.

An attempt was made to save something of the debacle over the Anglican–Methodist negotiations. The Churches Unity Commission issued Ten Propositions about Church Unity and referred them to its member Churches. In 1977 the General Synod accepted them as an acceptable basis for continued consultation with the other Churches which are partners in mission with the Church of England; but they got nowhere.

Attempts at reunion with non-episcopal Churches in England and Scotland have all ended in failure, although talks have started up again between Anglicans and Methodists. Meanwhile interest was moving towards a *rapprochement* with the Roman Catholic Church, with which a very different kind of courtship was simultaneously being conducted. The first personal introduction of the couple was the surprise visit of Archbishop Geoffrey Fisher to Pope John XXIII on 2 December 1960. There followed a further visit, when his successor Archbishop Michael Ramsey visited Paul VI, who gave him his episcopal ring! This might even have been construed as an engagement ring, as the relationship had greatly warmed. Would there be a marriage? Just as parents of a courting couple meet, so representatives of the Roman Catholic Church and Anglicans in 1969 began to meet in what is known as ARCIC, the Anglican–Roman Catholic International Commission. Unfudged agreed statements astonished the Churches; on the Eucharist in 1971; on the ministry in 1973, on authority in the Church in 1976 and 1981. The courtship was turning into a love affair. The final report on authority, which proposed a Universal Primacy, showed that there was still some way to go. Nonetheless some Roman Catholic priests anticipated the marriage by permitting Anglicans to receive Communion at their altars.

However, before an engagement could be announced, a menacing black cloud appeared on the horizon – the ordination of women as deacons and priests. It proved more or less the end of the affair. It was said to place a grave obstacle in the way of reunion. In 1982 Pope John Paul II visited England, and came to Canterbury Cathedral to a service of worship. He entered, as it were, on equal terms with Archbishop Runcie. He kissed all the Anglican diocesan bishops on both cheeks and seemed visibly impressed by the catholicity of the proceedings. Anglicans hoped that this would overcome his misgivings about the ordination of women. It was not to be. In 1984 General Synod decided to set up a working party to advise on legislation for their ordination. In 1992 many were surprised when all three houses of the General Synod (lay, priestly and episcopal) decided by a two-thirds majority that women could be ordained as priests. The cloud which had grown more and more menacing finally burst. The attitude of the Roman Catholic Church, whose ardour had been cooling during the process, now congealed into frost. The Pope, who was strongly opposed to the ordination of women to the priesthood, even ordered that there should be no *discussion* on the subject in the Roman Catholic Church. Although a second ARCIC has been appointed, no one expects much of it now. There has been recently another Commission set up to look at relations between Anglicans and the Roman Catholic Church. It has been greeted with good wishes, and it deserves support. A covenant was recently signed at Windsor in the presence of the Queen in which the mainstream churches in England committed themselves to achieving unity. While Churches have much to learn from one another, it must be said that there is no betrothal between the Anglican Communion and the Roman Catholic Church, and any proposal of marriage seems hopeless.

Meanwhile, the decision to ordain women produced a near schism in the Church of England which was only obviated by a non-theological device which would, I suppose, be described by the Orthodox Churches as 'the practice of economy'. Some churches refused the ministry of their diocesan bishops whose hands had been soiled by laying them on the heads of women at their ordination. Special bishops, commonly known as 'flying bishops', who disapproved of women's ordination were consecrated under the licence of the Archbishops of the two English provinces to minister to these parishes, in conjunction with the diocesan bishops concerned. These parishes are now urging the establishment of a non-territorial province in the Church of England to which they would belong. This would run counter to the catholic notions of what a diocese is, and would be tantamount to schism. If there are these difficulties within the Church of England, what chance can there be for reunion with the Roman Catholic Church?

Meanwhile trouble has been occurring in some evangelical parishes. Worried by ethical matters concerning the Church's attitude towards homosexual priests, and alleged laxity in doctrine, some parishes have been refusing to pay their assessed contribution to diocesan headquarters. There has even been a case of confirmations carried out by an overseas bishop in the diocese of one of the 'suspect' bishops. If matters are so difficult within the Church of England, what chance is there of its union with Churches which share these evangelicals' stance on such matters?

It must be said however that there has been some progress ecumenically between the Church of England and other Churches. It was agreed some time ago that communicant members in good standing of all Churches who subscribe to the doctrine of the Trinity be admitted to Holy Communion in the Church of England (Canon B 15 1 (b)). (One wonders what doctrine of the Trinity is intended here.) Negotiations have been re-opened with the Methodist Church in England and Wales, although no proposals have been forthcoming as yet. More lately, after negotiations with the Lutheran Church, intercommunion has been established between the two Churches, and full communion has been agreed with the Baltic Lutheran Churches. This is very welcome, but divided as we are by the expanse of the North Sea, it has little more than symbolic value. These are small gains compared with the failure of negotiations with other Churches from the middle of the last century until now.

Will the frost that has hardened formal relationships between the Church of England and the Roman Catholic Church turn into permafrost? It is difficult to say. It is not possible to see a way forward through the present impediments. It is conceivable that at some time in the future women may be ordained within the Roman Catholic Church, although it would be difficult for this to happen soon in view of the strong opposition of the present Pope. It is impossible to see any breakthrough on this matter with the Orthodox Churches, which abhor any change to their traditions (although the Romanian Orthodox Church, which recognizes Anglican orders, decided not to take any action when Anglicans ordained women). Again it is difficult to imagine a *rapprochement* between Roman Catholics and the Orthodox concerning the Roman claim to infallibility and to universal jurisdiction over the whole Church. The Orthodox reject this as strongly as Anglicans do. Although Pope John Paul II strongly desires a *rapprochement*, it is difficult to see this taking place, unless the Pope infallibly declares that he is not infallible, a ridiculous suggestion which belongs to cloud cuckoo land.

Furthermore, Anglicans reject both the dogma of the Immaculate Conception of Mary, 'infallibly' pronounced by Pius IX in 1849, and also the dogma of her bodily Assumption proclaimed by Pius XII in 1950. Although an Anglican is in no way forbidden to hold either or both of these doctrines, it is unthinkable that they should ever be required beliefs for members of the Anglican Communion, for there is no evidence in favour of either dogma either in the New Testament or in the tradition of the primitive Church. How can this seemingly impassable abyss ever be bridged? Once again, the only way I can think of is for the Pope infallibly to declare that they were not infallibly defined (a non-starter), or that they need only to be held symbolically (but symbolic of what?).

At least the Orthodox Churches are permitted by the Roman Catholic authorities to call themselves a Church. But according to the declaration *Dominus Iesus* in 2001 made by the Roman Catholic Congregation for the Doctrine of the Faith, and ratified and confirmed by the Pope, the Church of England is not a 'proper Church'. To explain what the reason is for this, it is necessary to return to the last century but one.

Pope Leo XIII in 1896 issued an Apostolic Letter known as *Apostolicae Curae*. This concluded that 'On our own initiative and with certain knowledge We pronounce and declare that ordinations performed according to the Anglican rite are utterly null and completely void.' The Commission appointed by the Pope was evenly divided for and against (ed. Franklin, 1996, p. 18). The Pope made his own decision, seemingly on grounds of ecclesiastical politics, hence the phrase 'on our own initiative' in his declaration. Although great efforts had been made in the Elizabethan Church to retain the apostolic succession of bishops, the Pope objected to the Church of England's sacramentality. Among other objections, his main point was that, in his judgement, the Anglican Ordinal revealed an intention to found a priesthood different from the 'sacrificing priesthood' of the Roman Catholic Church. Despite its erudite refutation by the two English Archbishops in their response *Saepius Officio*, this view seems to have persisted. But circumstances have changed. The Vatican archives of the period have been opened to inspection, the 'special place of Anglicanism' has been recognized in Vatican II's Decree on Ecumenism, the Pope gave Archbishop Ramsey his episcopal ring, and Rome has accepted the elucidations it sought on the ARCIC statements on Eucharist and Ministry. Now, surely, 100 years after *Apostolicae Curae* was issued, its views on Anglican Orders could be re-evaluated. This hope was clearly stated by members of ARCIC itself. It would seem, however, that the position remains as it was in 1896. In the absence of any other explanation, it would appear that, in Rome's judgement, once there is a wrong intention in the rite of ordination, the apostolic succession is irretrievably lost.

In the light of this the Church of England, apparently, is not regarded by the Roman Catholic Church as a proper Church. 'The ecclesial communities which have not preserved the valid Episcopate and the genuine and integral substance of the Eucharistic mystery are not Churches in the proper sense' (*Dominus Iesus*, 17). However, 'those who are baptized in these communities are, by Baptism, incorporated into Christ and thus are in a certain communion, albeit imperfect, with the Church'. Nonetheless, those ecclesial communities, although they contain 'many elements of sanctification and truth', at the same time 'derive their efficacy from the very fullness of grace and truth entrusted to the Catholic Church' (*Dominus Iesus*, 16).

There is no way, without submission on the part of the Church of England or a change of attitude on the part of the Roman Catholic Church, in which reconciliation between that Church and the Church of England can take place. There is not the slightest possibility of the Church of England agreeing to the allegation that it is not a Church in the proper sense. It is a Church, like every other Church, capable of sin and error, but it is fully convinced that, despite this, it is a proper Church. Again, I can see no possibility of the Church of England agreeing that it derives all its efficacy from the Roman Catholic Church: the very idea might be thought to be something of an insult.

I have recounted the ecumenical events which have taken place during my ministry in the Church of England, together with various failures and very limited successes in reunion negotiations. I have done this because my judgement on the future of ecumenism has inevitably been influenced by my own growing disappointment, not to say despair, of the process. Against this I must also place my very recent experience of ecumenism which I have enjoyed, thanks to the Focolare Movement. This movement began in an air raid shelter in Trent (in Italy) during the second World War, when the city was subjected to bombing from the Allied forces. Chiara Lubich is still its inspired and indefatigable leader; the movement is now both ecumenical and international, consisting of large numbers of men and women earning their keep in the secular world, but living together in Christian love. In addition to this, there are many 'Friends of the Focolare'. Chiara Lubich realized that her calling is to deepen internal Catholic unity, and to promote ecumenical unity among the Churches. She won the approval of Pope John Paul II, and also of the former Ecumenical Patriarch as well as Archbishop Ramsey who told her 'God's finger is in the movement'; and today it goes from strength to strength. Although I do not myself accept all the theology of the movement, I recognize the strength of its powerful spirituality and the spirit of Christian love that pervades all that it does.

Each year the Movement invites bishops who are friends of the Focolare to a kind of spiritual retreat and colloquy, at a different location each time. At the meeting which I attended at the Focolare 'Mariopolis' at Castel Gandolfo near Rome, and more recently near Zurich, there were bishops from many continents, and from many Churches; Roman Catholic, Anglican, Lutheran. Orthodox and Oriental Churches. Of course we did not share fully in each other's Eucharists (although we attended one of each), but in every other way we treated one another as equals, and even the Pope, when we had an audience with him, addressed us all as 'Venerable Bishops' without any distinction between those who belonged to a 'proper Church' and those who did not. Indeed the distinction seemed irrelevant at the time. During the time together, we went to the Catacombs, and each formally pronounced:

> United in the name of Jesus, we promise one another, that, for the rest of our lives we will strive in all things and above all things to love one another as Jesus loved us. Father, give us grace to live in such a way that each of us considers the other's

cross his own and the joy of one becomes the joy of the other, so that all may be one and the world may believe.

I have to say that, although I am sure that the sense of unity may well have been increased if we had enjoyed eucharistic hospitality from each other's Churches, the spiritual sense of unity actually outweighed sacramental unity. I know that small meetings of Christians often generate a strong dynamic of unity; but even taking that into account, the spiritual sense of unity, based on mutual Christian love, which is part of the Focolare spirituality, was extraordinary.

It is as I look back over this experience, and the failure of Christian attempts at reunion during the period of my ministry, that I have been forced to re-evaluate our striving for Christian reunion. (I must add that my present change of heart on the subject is not shared by the Focolare Movement itself.) I see no chance, humanly speaking, of reunion among the Protestant Churches and the Roman Catholic and Orthodox Churches, nor between the two latter Churches. I suppose some further reunion is conceivable between Protestant Churches (such as that achieved in the United Reformed Church, formed from Presbyterians and Congregationalists) and possibly a union between the Methodist and Anglicans (reuniting a schism which should never have taken place). But it is hard even to imagine reunion involving the Pentecostalist Churches, the non-Pentecostal Black Churches and what may be called the mainstream Churches. A friend told me of an interchurch walk on which she went, which involved prayers at both a Pentecostal and an Orthodox church. They both worshipped God through Jesus Christ, but their spiritualities were so different that she could not imagine them joining into one Church. The question then arises, is all this energy put into reunion really worth while? Are the thousands of hours involved well spent? It is wonderful that Christians of different denominations are beginning to tolerate one another. They are becoming friends, and beginning to co-operate in a spirit of amity and Christian love. It is marvellous that this is beginning to happen. But at the end of the day is it not sufficient, at least as things stand, to foster the ecumenical spirit within a Church and between Churches rather than seek reunion? It is difficult even to imagine what a totally reunited Christendom would look like.

Would it not be more productive and more in accordance with the Spirit of Christ to work for love, friendship and understanding between Churches rather than for their amalgamation in an organizational structure? Why cannot intercommunion between Churches be seen as a way of unity rather than its goal?

There would be certain pragmatic advantages. The spiritual should take precedence over the organizational. It is tragic to see the kind of opposition the Pope met from the Orthodox when he visited the Ukraine, or to hear of Independent Chapels leaving a local Council of Churches when the Roman Catholics join. If Christian priests, ministers and lay people were seen by the world to show real Christian love, acceptance and tolerance to members of other Churches or denominations, and actively to support them when this were needed, and so far as possible, to act together with them in matters such as social action, regardless of what Church they belonged to, would this not have far more impact on the world than reports of continuing failure to achieve institutional reunion between the major Churches?

Again, there could be grave disadvantages in one and one only huge world Church institution. The distance from a parish to the centre would be greater even than the distance felt between the Vatican authorities and those at the parochial level. There would be the probability of stifling centralization; and it is difficult even to consider what kind of central organization would be workable, nor (unless all who were baptized were recognized as members) on what kind of basis the Churches could agree to "reunion all round", other than that in Monsignor Ronnie Knox's famous satire on the subject. Various Churches have evolved their own traditions over the years, and of course they do not want to lose them. Although in the Roman Catholic Church uniate Churches do retain their traditions, they are still subject to the orders of the central authorities in Rome. What is the purpose of working towards something which one cannot even visualize?

It might be objected that, as with mergers in the commercial world, there would be savings of plant, overheads and perhaps human resources. But such mergers in the commercial world do not usually work to the benefit of an employee, and similarly they would probably not work to the benefit of lay people in the ecclesiastical world.

What of theology? There is an argument from the sacramental nature of the Church, according to which its outward and visible form should match its inner and spiritual nature. But, while it may be desirable to regard the Church as sacramental in this sense, there is no authority for so doing, and in any case, as we have seen its inner and spiritual nature is not, alas, one of spiritual unity, and until that occurs, it is useless to attempt visible reunion.

If we examine the Scriptures, we find that Jesus is never recorded as telling his disciples that they must act as one body. The Gospels record several disagreements among them. Few scholars believe that the so-called 'High Priestly Prayer' of Jesus contains the actual words of Jesus, but even if it does, Jesus prays for those who believe on him through the preaching of his followers 'that they all may be one; as thou, Father, art in me, and I in thee, that they also may be one in us: that the world may believe that thou hast sent me' (John 17.21 (AV)). But the union of the Father and the Son is anything but simple. There is certainly a spiritual unity between them, and it is of this that Jesus speaks, not organizational union. The Greek word used for 'one' in the quotation is the neuter *hen*, one thing, not the masculine form *heis* which would indicate identity. In St John's

Gospel the reason for unity is 'that the world may believe that thou hast sent me'. Certainly disunity detracts from the credibility of the Church. But Churches that were seen to be acting in love and charity, even if they remained distinct, would restore that credibility. Certainly if they were in sacramental as well as spiritual unity, this would help still more. I believe that the one would lead to the other.

Paul fervently exhorted his readers to unity, but it was to unity within a congregation, not the unity of different congregations. Certainly St Paul spoke of the Church collectively as a body, addressing himself mostly to a particular church (as in 1 Corinthians 12.12ff.) or to the Church as a whole (Coloss ians 1.18, 2.19 and Ephesians 4.4, 12). Since the human body is one organism composed of many members, so it can be argued that the universal Church is one body composed of many local congregations, and that it is therefore sinful to break up the one body into many parts. Dr J. A. T. Robinson wrote: 'It is impossible to exaggerate the materialism and crudity of Paul's doctrine of the Church as literally now the resurrection body of Christ' (Robinson, 1952, p. 51). Others (e.g. Best, 1955, p. 100) have strongly disagreed, regarding Paul's view of the body of Christ as a metaphor for the Church, similar to his metaphor of the building or the bride. There is little sign that Paul regarded all the congregations of Christians as composing one organism. Body was a very common metaphor in the Hellenistic milieu in which Paul wrote. He himself did not always agree with the church at Jerusalem, for example, over the question of Jewish Christians eating with Gentile Christians (Galatians 2.12); and he certainly did not take orders from the mother church at Jerusalem. But that did not prevent him from enjoying a spiritual unity with its leaders (Galatians 2.9) and even organizing a collection from all the churches to whom he was ministering for the mother church when it was in need.

I recognize that it is possible to read into these biblical

passages a call to all the Churches for reunion, but another interpretation, as I have attempted to show, seems to me more probable; and if that be so, there is no objection, from a biblical point of view, to concentrating on the spiritual unity of the Churches rather than engaging in futile attempts at reunion.

5

Disestablishment?

When I became a Christian in my teens, I had to decide in which Church I would be baptized. I became a member of the Church of England not because I thought that it was the best Church – how could I know the differences between any of the Churches in the UK? – but because I just wanted to be an ordinary Christian in England, and so it seemed to follow that I should be a member of the Church of England. That was well over half a century ago. At that time the Church of England had a far larger constituency than it does now. A larger proportion of the populace attended church, and the Church of England had the largest attendances. Today things have changed. The Roman Catholic Church has a great problem on its hands in this country, with its very small number of ordinands (already there are parishes without priests, and it is reckoned that their number is likely to double in 15–20 years): its mass attendance and its solemnization of marriage have dramatically decreased in the last half century. Nonetheless so far as normal Sunday attendance is concerned it is now slightly ahead of the Church of England. In this period large numbers have immigrated into the UK, and among them are a good number of Roman Catholics; so the Church of England is no longer the Church which has on a Sunday the greatest number of worshippers. The fact that the Roman Catholic Church is no longer so inward-looking and has a greater involvement in social and political affairs further dilutes the impact of the Church of England on society.

This influx has added greatly to our culture and is to be welcomed. At the same time it has altered the religious complexion of our land, especially in London and Birmingham and other large cities where these immigrants have mostly settled. It would not be correct to regard this country as a multifaith society, for Christians, many of whom no doubt are very nominal, far outnumber Jews, Muslims, Hindus, Sikhs and Buddhists living in the UK. But their presence does mean that the Christian faith can no longer be considered a near monopoly here.

Sects multiply, and modern methods of advertising can make them attractive. Furthermore, for the first time many white English people, who in the past have known no other religion than the Christian faith, are brought up against the faith of neighbours who belong to a different religion which is often more vibrantly held than their own faith. There is a large amount of movement from one religion to another. It is even claimed that a thousand people a day change their faith in the UK (Romain, 2000, p. 2).

Even more important, there is increasing secularism. Although many admit to a spiritual vacuum and are seeking to fill it, the mainstream Churches have a decreasing credibility to more and more people. This particularly affects the Established Church, as all aspects of the Establishment – whether it be royalty, or Church, or parliament or the judiciary – carry less and less authority to an increasing number of the population. These changes are beginning to make me change my views which I have held over many years. In the past I have strongly supported the Established Church from the attacks of disestablishmentarians. Today I am by no means so sure. Sometimes second thoughts are better than first thoughts. I am by no means the only person to have had second thoughts on this subject. Bishop Hensley Henson of Durham began by being a stalwart upholder of the Established Church. But after the passing of the Enabling Act he changed his mind, and was in favour of disestablishment.

We are concerned with the situation as it is today. But to

understand how the Established Church has come about, it is necessary to go back a millennium and a half in English history. The establishment of the Church in England began long ago. Christians existed in this country from about AD 200; but the mission of St Augustine, sent from Rome, in AD 597 began the conversion of England. When there was a clash between Roman and Celtic tradition, the issue was decided in favour of Rome in AD 663 by the King.

> In Anglo-Saxon times the boundary between Church and State was far less clearly drawn than it has been in more recent days. The king was regarded not only as head of the Church, but as 'the vicar of Christ among Christian folk', a title which he could never have claimed after the rise of papal power in the eleventh century. Practically all appointments to bishoprics and abbeys were made by the king himself. (Moorman, 1953, p. 47)

After the Norman conquest in 1066, William brought the Church in England into the mainstream of church life, but he insisted, under threat of excommunication by the Pope, on keeping the English Church under his own control. No one could be excommunicated without the king's consent, no bishop could go abroad without his permission, and no papal letter could be received until William had read it! However, Anselm, Archbishop of Canterbury, an Italian like his predecessor, broke the independence of the kings of England and gave the papacy greater control over the English Church than it had ever had before. Fierce battles ensued between the king and the Church for many years, notably in the confrontation between Henry II and Becket which ended in his martyrdom, and in John's rejection of papal authority which resulted in England being placed under an interdict. In the fourteenth century the state passed a series of acts on the basis that the power of the papacy in England ought to be diminished.

Disestablishment?

The Reformation in the sixteenth century decisively ended the power of the papacy over the Church in England when Henry VIII made himself, by Act of Parliament, head of the Church. But this was foreshadowed in earlier centuries in battles between the king and the Church. Ever since, the Church of England has been established, that is to say, it has been subject to the state and singled out for special regulation by Acts of Parliament. This is clearly different from the New Testament conception of the Church. According to St Paul the power of the state must be respected, but it has no part in the governance of the Church. But the situation was entirely different in those early days. The Church began as a sect of the Jewish religion. Its adherents refused to burn incense at an Emperor's shrine. Far from being governed by the state, it became the object of persecution by the state during the reigns of successive Roman Emperors until the time of Constantine the Great, who made Christianity the established religion of the Roman Empire and exercised great influence over the Church.

Here in England the establishment of the Church has continued through all the vicissitudes which it has suffered, both during its forcible return to Roman obedience under Queen Mary, the daughter of Henry VIII's first (Roman Catholic) wife, under the Reformation Settlement of Queen Elizabeth I, and even through the period of the Commonwealth, despite episcopally ordained clergy being ejected from their parishes, and the introduction of non-liturgical worship. Religion remained established at the Restoration of monarchical government under Charles II, and again, after the demise of the Stuarts, at the 'Glorious Revolution' under William and Mary. And the Established Church continues to this day.

In the past, although great good was done by the Established Church, much injustice has also occurred. The Reformation Settlement was intended to make the Church of England the Church of all the English people. There was a time when

Roman priests were killed under Queen Elizabeth (mostly for treason, because the Pope had demanded her downfall) and Roman Catholics were fined for non-attendance at Anglican churches. The so-called 'Free Churches' enjoyed no liberty at all. Non-Anglicans could not attend universities, and they could not hold offices of state. (Jews, permitted from the time of Cromwell to enter Britain and to worship in a synagogue, were subject to similar prohibitions.) It was only gradually that more liberal policies were introduced. By today all such injustices have been removed. The only remaining restriction, introduced at the 'Glorious Revolution' when the Roman Catholic King James II fled the country, concerns the legal ban on the marriage of members of the Royal Family in line to the throne to a Roman Catholic spouse. The monarch, since the time of Elizabeth I, has been the 'supreme governor' of the Church of England.

Because of the monarch's status in the Church (even though the role of supreme governor is now discharged by the Prime Minister), there is a special relationship between her and the bishops and clergy of the Established Church. Before taking up office a bishop has to do homage in the presence of the Home Secretary, putting his hands over those of the monarch, and swearing allegiance in the words of a sixteenth-century oath, that 'no foreign prelate or potentate hath any jurisdiction in this realm of England'. Furthermore the clergy of the Church of England, and other church officers, before taking up office in the Church are required to take an Oath of Allegiance to the monarch.

In turn the monarch has to take a corresponding Oath about them at the commencement of the Coronation Service, as follows:

> *Archbishop*: Will you to the utmost of your power maintain the Laws of God and the true profession of the Gospel? Will you to the utmost of your power maintain in the United Kingdom the Protestant Reformed Religion established by law? Will you

maintain and preserve inviolably the settlement of the Church of England, and the doctrine, worship, discipline and government thereof, as by law established in England? And will you preserve unto the Bishops and Clergy of England, and to the Churches committed to their charge, all such rights and privileges, as by law do or shall appertain to them or any of them?

Queen: All this I promise to do.

The Queen then goes to the Altar, and takes a solemn Oath to observe these promises; laying the right hand on the Holy Gospel in the great Bible and saying these words:

The things which I have here before promised, I will perform and keep. So help me God.

The Queen shall kiss the Book and sign the Oath. (Ratcliffe, 1953, p. 38)

The words of the Act of Homage and the Oath of Allegiance could be dispensed with in a disestablished Church. The words of the Coronation Service have been amended many times for different coronations, and doubtless they could be amended again. If the Church of England were to be disestablished, the whole of the section cited above could be omitted.

I pointed out some time ago that it would be difficult for the monarch to give royal assent to any Bill promoting disestablishment after having sworn such a solemn oath to preserve inviolably the Established Church; and if such a Bill were to be passed in both Houses of Parliament, a crisis could occur, with a constitutional monarch (who is supposed to do what he or she is told by Parliament) refusing to give royal assent to a Bill agreed in both Houses (or perhaps in the House of Commons only, by virtue of the Parliament Act). In fact, I suggested that the only time that disestablishment could take place would be in the period between the accession of a monarch and the Coronation Oath, since the previous monarch would be bound by the word of the oath already taken. However, Queen Victoria, despite her oath to maintain inviolably the settlement of the United Church of England and Ireland, had no apparent problem in agreeing to the Bill disestablishing the Church of Ireland (Buchanan, 1994, p. 148). But conscience cannot be determined by precedent. Rather like the Nonjurors who refused a new Oath of Allegiance to William and Mary after the flight of James II, the conscience of a monarch who refused the royal assent on the grounds outlined above should be respected.

If the Church of England were disestablished, the 1701 law that forbids an heir to the throne from marrying a Roman Catholic would presumably be repealed. Such a move is dear to the hearts of many Roman Catholics who consider it unfair religious discrimination, and a movement is afoot for its repeal. On the other hand, there is a problem. Although the Roman regulation has been rescinded which required a non-Roman spouse to sign a piece of paper to the effect that any children of the marriage will be brought up as Roman Catholics, the Roman spouse is still required to state that he or she will, to the utmost of their endeavours, ensure that any children are brought up as Roman Catholics. It is natural that children should share their mother's faith, since mothers have most to do with their upbringing. So if a male heir to the throne were to marry a Roman Catholic, in all probability their children would become Roman Catholics, and Britain would henceforth have a Roman Catholic monarchy. This might well be against the wishes of the populace.

In the passage from the Coronation Service cited above, the Church of England is described as established according to the law of the land. Establishment has been described as 'just a word, and an ambiguous one at that' (Avis, 2001, p. 87). Certainly it can be used with varying shades of meaning, but, so far as the Church of England is concerned, it is best defined as the body of laws which affects the Church of England but not other Churches, and which results in the state having ultimate control, despite having given the Church freedom to decide (within limits) its own liturgies, discipline and doctrine. No doubt Parliament, if it were so minded, could pass laws which only affect other particular Churches in England, but it doesn't. But it does include among the many laws that it makes those which only affect the Church of England. Over the years so many laws of this kind have been passed that, it has been said, it would take a whole session of Parliament to reverse them all. Furthermore, the state has ultimate control over the appointments of bishops.

The existence of these laws bestows on the Church of England a privileged position, and gives the impression to many that the Church of England only exists because it is propped up by the state. But it is most certainly not propped up with state money. The Church of England has its own endowments which are not nearly enough to pay its expenses, and increasing sums have to be provided by its lay members in order to keep it solvent. Other Established Churches, such as Churches in Germany, have a church tax which is collected by the state. There is no such church tax for the Church of England. It does not receive one penny from the state, except for services for which other denominations can also receive money; for the maintenance of ancient buildings (from the National Heritage Fund), and for the services of chaplains in the National Health Service, the Armed Services and the Prison Service. The argument for and against an Established Church does not rest upon financial matters, unless disendowment were to follow upon disestablishment, which is possible but improbable.

There is a very long history of an Established Church in England, and in any country that values tradition there is likely to be a strong reluctance on the part of many people to put an end to such an ancient tradition. It is one thing to set up a constitution like that of the United States of America, which rejected the idea of an Established Church: it is quite another to disestablish a Church that has been established for almost as long as England, as we know it, has existed. The main reason for retaining it, as I used to think in the past, is that if the Church of England were disestablished, it would appear to the people of England that this country had officially disowned the Christian faith, and that England was now avowedly a fully secular country. An Archbishop wrote 50 years ago: 'Disestablishment at this time would be regarded as the national repudiation of Christianity, and its effects would be felt far beyond the borders of the Church' (Garbett, 1959, p. 315). For the past 50 years I have agreed with that wholeheartedly. Furthermore, there is no strong move for disestablishment in the Church, among minority religions, or in the country as a whole.

Apart from this argument from tradition, there are other arguments in favour of continuing the establishment of the Church of England. It marks the 'importance of the formal and structural recognition of the affairs of God in the constitution of the state' (Avis, 2001, p. 12), although this is given scant recognition today in the mass media. It also affords ceremonies which can embody public grief or joy (although it would be possible for these to take place without an Established Church, e.g., in a ceremony of coronation in conjunction with other Churches, or as today on Commonwealth Day in Westminster Abbey, with the participation of other religious bodies).

More importantly, under the Elizabethan settlement membership of the Church of England was intentionally drawn very wide. The Church, officially described in the later Coronation Oath as the Protestant Reformed Religion, contains in the reign of Elizabeth II (as it did in the days of Elizabeth I) a strong catholic element. It has retained the catholic ministry, the catholic Eucharist, the catholic episcopate, the catholic calendar and catholic worship. The Church of England has sometimes been described as a Church with Protestant Articles and a catholic liturgy. It has also contained down the centuries a strong liberal element; Latitudinarians, Broad Churchmen, Modern Churchmen, liberals, whatever they may be called. They are still there, though somewhat eclipsed at the moment. The Church has a high regard for sound learning and a reasoned approach to theology. In this sense it is a deliberately inclusive Church in which Christian fellowship, which includes sacramental fellowship, is deemed more important than doctrinal uniformity. It was intended to be the Church for all English men and women (although it failed in this aim). It is no longer a Church of strict uniformity in worship. While the Book of Common Prayer always remains an option for any parish whose council desires it to be used, the new prayer book *Common Worship* legalizes a very large number of options and offers great flexibility in the content of worship. This breadth of churchmanship might well be more difficult to maintain in a disestablished Church. Establishment helps to keep the Church from a narrow inward-looking sectarianism (although in some more extreme evangelical parishes this does not seem to be the case).

Because the Church of England is the Established Church, its parishes include everyone in the country, and every person living in a parish has rights in the parish church, whatever their style of churchmanship may be. She or he may attend worship there (though few do), and has a right to have their children baptized there, to be married there (according to canon law whether they are baptized or not) and a right to have a funeral service in the parish church before burial or cremation. The fact that few exercise these rights does not mean that they are unimportant. The Church of England is not a sect for its adherents: as the Established Church, it is there to be of service to the surrounding community. The vicar or rector of a parish can in principle call on any and every family within the parish. (I say in principle because the large numbers in many parishes make this impossible to achieve.) The incumbent also has a certain standing in the community. This standing still holds good in the rural areas of the country; but it must be admitted that during the last century it has been greatly lessened in many urban areas, although the Church of England parson is often the only servant of the local community who actually lives within the parish. In the inner city doctors, police, social workers, and teachers usually commute from outside the area, and they probably cannot live in some of the outer suburbs because they cannot afford the price of housing there. The Church of England, with its vicarage adjacent to a church, maintains a priest within the parish. The Free Churches have largely withdrawn from the inner city, and the Roman Catholic Church with its large parishes often has no priest resident nearby.

The inclusiveness of the Established Church may mean a blurring of the boundaries between the committed and the uncommitted, but it is a symbol that the Christian faith is for everyone, and not just for the chosen few. There is a certain fringe of people who are neither committed nor uncommitted, who attend church perhaps at Christmas and possibly at Easter, who regard themselves as Christians even though their knowledge of Christianity is rudimentary. They may once have been more committed, but they have somewhat drifted away; yet they do not like to think of themselves as agnostic. They are aware of the difference between right and wrong, they respect Christ, and they believe that conduct matters, and that Christianity helps to keep people on the rails. There are those committed Christians who believe that people should either be 'in' or 'out' of the Church, and no doubt they disapprove of this fringe. On the other hand, God loves everyone equally, and there is room for all in the Church in the hope that its channel of grace may irradiate their lives.

Disestablishment?

Church of England schools are part of the state structure. Whether their status be 'aided' or 'controlled', these church schools are extremely popular in the community. Originally most of them were built as a contribution by the Church to education at a time before primary schooling became compulsory and was provided free by the state. They were not built, like Roman Catholic schools, as part of a strategy for creating the local congregation. Although nowadays Church of England church schools have so many applicants that they have to give Christian families some priority, most of them also keep places for other children, especially the disadvantaged in the local community. There is no sense in which they can be called sectarian schools. When I was in Birmingham, I found that church primary schools were very popular among Muslim families, because they felt that at least there would be some teaching about God. They are a further symbol of the inclusiveness of the Established Church. What is more, they are not only popular, but they also score high on the official league table of schools; and the government has recently endorsed the view that there should be many more of these at secondary level.

In the Church of England during the last century there has been taking place what might be called 'creeping disestablishment'. The Convocations of the clergy which had been in abeyance for centuries were revived; and canon law, which is legally binding on the clergy and which must not clash with statute law, was revised. A Church Assembly (in which women as well as men can be elected) was introduced. The Life and Liberty movement after the first Great War bore fruit in the formation of parochial church councils to work with the incumbent in managing local church affairs and dealing with the maintenance of fabric and finance. The Church Assembly could pass Measures, but they have to be approved by Parliament before they become law, after having earlier gained the approval of an Ecclesiastical Committee formed from both

Houses. (This Committee has lately been flexing its muscles.) Although the Convocations occasionally meet separately, they and the Church Assembly have joined to form the General Synod, consisting of the three Houses of Laity, Clergy and the Bishops. It decides on strategy for the Church put forward by the Archbishops' Council, and forms a sounding board for matters affecting the state as well as the Church. Local synods also exist at deanery and diocesan levels. The Worship and Doctrine Measure permits the Church to be in charge of its own liturgy, providing that the Book of Common Prayer always remains an option for worship.

As for the appointment of bishops, every diocese has a Vacancy in See Committee which informs the Crown Appointments Commission when there is a vacancy about its views concerning the appointment of the next bishop, and may even forward names. The Crown Appointments Commission, which consists of an Archbishop, clergy and lay members, is entirely appointed by the Church (except on the appointment of the Archbishop of Canterbury when the chairperson is appointed by the Prime Minister). The Committee presents two names to the Crown, and if neither of these are acceptable, it presents a further two names. It is thought that this has happened only once. Surprisingly, the Church has not pressed for the presentation of only one name rather than two, but seems strangely content with the present situation.

The Church Commissioners is a body set up by Parliament, whose First Estates Commissioner is appointed by the Crown. It is a body separate from the Church, and it is responsible for the stewardship of all the Church's capital finances. For all the good work that it has done, in the recent past there have been catastrophic mistakes made by the Commissioners with the result that they have taken on more financial responsibilities than they can discharge, and their actuaries have failed to realize that clergy, like the rest of the population, are living longer lives and so their pension responsibilities are far greater than they had thought. As a result dioceses are faced with finding huge new sums of money: the diocese in which I live has to find an extra £1,500,000 in a single year. Lately the Commissioners have been relieved of the responsibility for distributing their investment income to dioceses, and the Archbishops' Council has taken this over. The Commissioners must be regarded as part of the Establishment, though not part of the Established Church. No one can be sure what will happen to the capital sums that they hold in the event of disestablishment. When the Church in Wales was disestablished, part of their capital went to the funding of museums! However, that Church was known to be a minority Church in the Principality, and it is very unlikely that the same fate would await the Church of England's massive endowments. If the Church of England were to be disestablished, the Church Commissioners would be likely to remain as a body charged with the Church's capital in the form of churches, buildings and finances, but it would no longer be a body whose officers are appointed through the Crown.

It is apparent that the Church of England has come a long way towards self-government. But not all the way. Its bishops are still appointed by the Crown, and its legislation (other than canon law, which requires the Royal Assent) has to have the approval of Parliament before it becomes law. What difference would it make to the Church of England if it were disestablished?

The Church would be able to appoint its own bishops without reference to the Crown. This would end the accusation that bishops are still political appointments, even though now the Church selects two names and the Crown appoints one of them. I was the first bishop to be appointed by this (comparatively) new system first introduced over 30 years ago. At that time the system leaked terribly, despite the vows of all concerned to maintain strict confidentiality. The result was some unpleasantness for me, as the local media, on grounds of my environmental views, joined with others to try to prevent my appointment when it became known that I was a candidate. For that reason I regret the more open system of appointment recently proposed by a church committee, as I fear it may lead to further unpleasantnesses for those known to be candidates. It is sometimes said that the Crown makes better appointments than the Church. Now that the Church selects the names, that argument no longer holds water, if it ever did.

One of the privileges of the Established Church is that its two Archbishops and 24 of its bishops sit in the House of Lords. Apart from the two Archbishops and the 'Prince Bishops' (London, Durham and Winchester) who sit there by right, the remainder come into the Lords by seniority, waiting for bishops to retire or die. (Of my nine years as a diocesan bishop, I was in the Lords for only three, owing to a lack of retirements or deaths.) If bishops still remain there when the future constitution of the House is decided, some other means of appointment other than by seniority of tenure will have to be devised, since some bishops might never get into the Lords, and others would sit for such a short time that they could not be of much use.

Naturally there is a feeling that clergy other than Anglican bishops should be there. However, Moderators of the Kirk and Presidents of the Methodist Conference are appointed on an annual basis, and other Free Church senior clergy hold appointments for only a limited period. Roman Catholic bishops are not permitted by their Church to take part in politics. It is difficult to see how clergy of other denominations could be made members, except on an individual basis. In any case Anglican diocesan bishops only qualify for membership of the legislature because they are appointed by the Crown, which would cease if there were disestablishment.

Do the bishops really contribute much to the Lords? Certainly they have always been there. (The government's side of the House is known as the Bishops' because they all used to sit there.) We have been made very welcome there, but as I look back over the years I do not think that bishops have achieved much. This is partly due to the fact that a bishop's diary is made up a year ahead, and the House of Lords' only a month ahead; and a bishop cannot cancel long-standing engagements to attend. So very few bishops attend debates, other than to say prayers for a week at the beginning of the day's session. The only important change in a Bill made by a bishop that I can remember was an amendment by Monsignor Graham Leonard when he was the Anglican Bishop of London, and chairman of Synod's Board of Education: it made an important difference to an Education Bill. I once proposed a Bill in the Lords. It was a modest affair to prevent the abortion of a foetus that was capable of being born alive. When I asked the Leader of the House, Lord Denham, if someone could be found to promote such a Bill, he said: 'Why not yourself?' When I replied that bishops never introduce Bills, he sent for the Clerk of Parliaments who told him that a bishop had introduced a Bill a long time ago, concerning, if I remember aright, drains or the like. So I went ahead and got my Bill through Second Reading, but then I had to retire from the House at the end of my tenure as a Diocesan. On another occasion I opposed a Bill which would have legalized Sunday trading. It failed in the Commons, but in the Lords there was such a built-in majority in favour of the Bill that opposition was hopeless. (A similar Bill later became law.) Naturally one would be sorry to have missed the privilege of being a member of the House of Lords, but I do not think that the country would be worse off if bishops no longer sat there by right. If that came to pass, presumably the ban on clergy standing for membership of the House of Commons would be removed.

The other main difference that disestablishment would make would be the requirement that any Measure passed by the General Synod has to go to the Ecclesiastical Committee of

Parliament, and then to the two Houses (which can then only pass or reject the Measure, but cannot amend it). A glance at Hansard when church debates take place in the Commons shows that very few people speak, or indeed are present; and the few that do often mount their hobby-horse. Occasionally Measures passed by the General Synod have, as a result of the Ecclesiastical Committee's remarks, been slightly improved. But the country (or indeed the Church of England) would not be worse off if the Church of England could manage its affairs without the intrusion of Parliament.

If the Church of England were disestablished, this should not affect the status or position of church schools, which are held on different trusts from those of the Church. The Church would be in full charge of its own affairs and would appoint its own bishops without any state interference. It should still remain a broad Church, with a large spectrum of churchmanship. Although parishioners would no longer have legal rights in their parish church unless they were on its electoral roll, they would still be welcome there. Bishops would presumably not be in the House of Lords, but they would have more time for their dioceses and for the welfare of all who live in them. At the parish level, the situation would be the same as it is now.

The arguments I have mustered in favour of an Established Church are strong; but two factors are changing my mind about the desirability of disestablishment.

The first is the low esteem in which all aspects of the Establishment are now held by the general public; the monarchy, the Houses of Parliament, the judiciary and the Church of England. The Establishment is generally thought to be out-of-date, stuffy, and unsuited to contemporary Britain. The monarchy has been the subject of much criticism, partly because of marital disasters, partly because of allegedly high costs. The Houses of Parliament are to a great extent ignored. At the last general election, millions abstained from voting, and the present government seems to respect the media more than Parliament. Allegations of sleaze have lowered its repute, and the treatment by MPs of its Parliamentary Commissioner for Standards has made it, in the words of *The Times* newspaper, a 'house of ill repute'. The House of Lords is in a strange state of transition, with most hereditary peers excluded. Proposals about its future seem to put even more patronage in the hands of a Prime Minister. The judiciary is also criticized, as can be seen by the threat of fixed sentences which will remove a judge's discretion. The Church would gain rather than lose in respect and credibility if it asked for disestablishment. With an Anglican Prime Minister and many key members of his government known to be Christians, disestablishment would not appear to be a repudiation by the state of Christianity. The Christian faith would not be degraded in any way by such a move. The legitimate grievances of other Churches in the land would be removed. Like its sister Church in Wales, which has been disestablished, there would be little change in the Church of England's membership or in its pastoral ministry. The Church could settle its own affairs, and there would be no place for the accusation of Erastianism.

The second reason why I now believe that it should be disestablished is because of its annually decreasing numbers. Fewer children are being baptized, 21 per cent of infants under 1 in the latest figures. Fewer people are being confirmed, 39,000 in 1998, the most recent figures. In the same year, only 26 per cent of all marriages took place in the Church of England, a number affected by the new laws concerning the licensing of places for secular weddings. Divorce is more and more common; and so is abortion. Out of a population of some 50,000,000 in England, only 1,500,000 have declared themselves members of the Church of England by enlisting on its electoral rolls. In 1999 (the latest figures available as I write) the number of Christmas communicants was 1,308,000: Easter communicants were less than that, 1,192,700, not much more than 2 per cent. As for usual Sunday attendance, this was as low as 968,800, under one million. The Church of England can still maintain its thousands of churches and pay its thousands of clergy – just. It is still a force to be reckoned with, and retains the affections of many. The press, which is generally hostile to the Church of England, reports (without any actual monitoring of its worship) that thousands are deserting its pews, but this is not the case. But there is a persistent if gradual decrease in attendance. Nowadays missionaries are coming here from abroad from the very countries to which we once sent our own missionaries!

A case can be made for an Established Church when only a minority of the population attends its services; but there comes a cut-off point when only a very small percentage attend church. Have we reached such a point, or are we very close to reaching it? There is a general increase in consumerism and materialism in the country as a whole. The media pay less and less attention to the Churches. Christianity now has little impact on modern culture and intellectual life. Only Archbishops can gain a hearing in the mass media, and that not always. Dr George Carey, when Archbishop of Canterbury, said that a tacit atheism prevails. The Cardinal Archbishop of Westminster, in a strange phrase, said that, as a backdrop to people's lives, Christianity had almost been vanquished. Advertisements now feel free to use the clergy and the Church in a manner which is quite inappropriate. Although religious education is supposed to be taught in all state schools, it has a low priority and is often honoured more in the breach than in the observance of the law. Ask many young people about Christianity, and you find a *tabula rasa*: they know nothing at all, or what they do know is a gross distortion of the truth. We are no longer a Christian country. We are not yet unChristian, but we are, alas, at the moment post-Christian. There is a general breakdown of the values which have derived from Christianity.

Disestablishment?

This makes it an exhilarating time to be a Christian. But in these circumstances, is it still appropriate for the Church to be 'established by law'? Disestablishment would in no way impede its mission or its ministry, but it could well add to its credibility.

6

Other Religions

One of the most pressing problems facing the Church is to define, and in some cases to redefine, its position with other faiths. There was a time in the last century when the Christian Church had more or less a monopoly in the UK. There were small minorities of Jews and those of other faiths, but their number did not compare with that of Christians. Now the position has altered. This is partly the result of globalization, but mostly because of the large numbers of Hindus, Sikhs, Muslims and adherents of other faiths who have immigrated to these islands. Gurdwaras, mosques and Hindu and even Buddhist temples now exist in most big cities. As these immigrants become integrated into our multicultural society, ordinary people find themselves alongside them. They discover that these more recent newcomers are ordinary people like themselves, and that they often take their religion more seriously than they have done. They are puzzled.

In the past members of other faiths were often classed as 'heathens'. Fundamentalist Christians thought that they would go to hell when they died. However, this was not a general view. In fact, there was no general view. The relationship of Christianity to other faiths was for most people (except for missionaries and their supporters) an academic problem which did not concern them. But now it has become a personal puzzle for many individual Christians. People of other faiths often have strongly held moral views, they bring up their families very conscientiously, they may have a transcendental experience of God and they seem to lead lives no worse than that of the average

Christian. They worship God – surely the same God as Christians worship? It is no longer possible for most people to believe that they will go to hell, while Christians go to heaven. But that in itself does not solve our problem. Are all religions really the same? What is the relationship between other people's faith and that of Christians?

The Roman Catholic Church has changed its view about this more than on any other subject. The doctrine *extra ecclesia nulla salus* – no salvation outside the Church – at first referred simply to the Roman Catholic Church: its members alone could find salvation. Then the term was extended to include other Churches, and then those who have *fides informis*, an unformed faith. The final change came at the Second Vatican Council, where it is stated that 'in Hinduism men contemplate the divine mystery and express it through an unspent fruitfulness of myths and through searching philosophical enquiry'. Buddhism 'teaches a path by which men, in a devout and confident spirit, can either reach a state of absolute freedom or attain supreme enlightenment through their own efforts or by higher assistance'. 'Other religions to be found everywhere strive variously to answer the restless searchings of the human heart.' As for the Abrahamic faiths, Muslims 'along with us adore the one and merciful God' and the Jews 'still remain most dear to God' (*Nostra Aetate* 2, 3, 4).

How do the Roman Catholic authorities reconcile this positive attitude to other faiths while at the same time maintaining that Christ is the way, the life and the truth? The recent Declaration *Dominus Iesus* is concerned with the 'unicity and salvific universality of Jesus Christ and the Church'. Although it received notoriety on account of its assertion that most non-Roman Churches are not 'proper Churches', in fact the main thrust of the Declaration is concerned with that Church's relationship to other religions. The Declaration cites the decree *Unitatis Redintegratio* that 'the Church, a pilgrim now on earth, is necessary for salvation: the one Christ is the mediator and the way of salvation'. This seems to imply that adherents of other religions are outside the sphere of salvation. But the Declaration goes on to quote from another decree of the Second Vatican Council about those who are not formal or visible members of the Church:

> Salvation in Christ is accessible by virtue of a grace which, while having a mysterious relationship with the Church, does not make them formally part of the Church, but enlightens them in a way which is accommodated to their spiritual and material situation. This grace comes from Christ: it is the result of his sacrifice and is communicated by the Holy Spirit. (*Ad Gentes*, 2)

How can this happen? According to *Ad Gentes*, 'God bestows this grace in ways known to himself' (*Ad Gentes*, 7). In other words, we do not know how it happens. But if we are ignorant about the mode by which this grace is given through the sacrifice of Christ, then how can we know that it is through Christ's sacrifice that the grace is bestowed, unless we are dogmatically certain that this is the only way in which this grace could be bestowed? It is just this dogmatic certainty that the Roman Catholic Church asserts when it affirms that 'it would be contrary to the faith to consider the Church as *one way* of salvation alongside those constituted by the other religions, seen as complementary to the Church or substantially equivalent to her, even if these are said to be converging with the Church towards the eschatological Kingdom of God' (*Dominus Iesus*, 21).

How can the two concepts, the unique sacrifice of Christ and more or less universal salvation, be logically held together without paradox? The only way, so far as I can see, would be to hold that Christ's unique sacrifice is an *opus operatum*, an objective act by which atonement was made for the sins of the whole world, whether people are aware of this or not, whether or not they repent, and whether or not they have faith. But such a view would be contrary to the basic Christian belief that it is through faith that we are saved. Furthermore, it would be a strange sacrifice for Jesus to make, almost as though God, having brought the universe into being in which human beings have evolved, needed to have a sacrifice in order to generate the grace which would bring people back on course. A sacrifice to whom? To himself?

One must ask whether it is reasonable to affirm that members of other faiths, who may be respectful of Christianity but who reject Christ as their Saviour, are nonetheless saved precisely through the saving grace which comes from Christ. Members of other faiths could never accept this, and they might well regard such a view as insulting their integrity.

On the other hand, there are those who are relativists. They believe that the Christian faith is only one path to the Ultimate, while other ways are equally valid. The most eloquent exponent of this view is Professor John Hick. He holds that the various religions of the world give cultural expression to their faith and experience of Ultimate Reality about whom (or about which) nothing is known other than its benign existence. He explains his position as follows:

> When we see the different religious cultures as diverse contexts in terms of which the universal presence of the Ultimate is differently appropriated, we cease to be perplexed by their apparently conflicting teachings. For it is possible to use very different sets of concepts and images, with very different communal and historical resonances, to speak about the benign (from our point of view) character of the Ultimate, about the total claim and gifts that its presence constitutes for our lives, and about the inner transformation from self-centredness towards a radically new orientation centred on the ultimately Real. (Hick, 1989, p. 43)

It is certainly true that cultural elements affect people's beliefs and practice. But this theory of religions does not always work out in practice. My own conversion to the Christian faith is not explained by the theory that religions are the expression of different cultures: it does not explain why, as a Jew, I became a Christian in twentieth-century British culture, while other Jews, living in the same culture, did not. The Christian faith spread to the East as well as to the West but the cultures of both are very different from the Middle Eastern culture where it began. The expression of the Christian faith differs in the East from that in the West, in its liturgies and to some extent in its beliefs, due, no doubt, to cultural influences; but it is the same Christian faith. Further, I do not think that some of the major differences between diverse faiths (e.g., whether God is to be addressed personally or whether he is impersonal) can be satisfactorily explained on this hypothesis.

The matter may perhaps be better approached by quite another route which preserves the uniqueness of Christ, and which also extends the loving acceptance by God to members of other faiths. The Roman Catholic view makes all depend on the sacrifice of Christ. But just what does this mean? The doctrine of the atonement does not appear in any Christian creed. The Apostles' Creed simply records Jesus's death. The so-called Nicene Creed records it too, but earlier it affirms that 'for us and for our salvation [he] came down from heaven . . .'. This seems to imply that it was not so much the sacrifice of Christ that brings us salvation as his incarnation. If we understand by atonement 'at-one-ment', we might say that, according to the Creed, it was through the incarnation that we are made at one with God.

In the New Testament the event of Jesus is interpreted through a great variety of images. It is described as forgiving, healing, rescuing from the domain of darkness, liberating by payment of a ransom, sealing a pledge, justifying, consecrating, electing, redeeming (as in the Roman custom whereby a freed slave was 'bought back' by a god through money paid into the temple treasury), atoning, expiating, reconciling, cleansing, incorporating into Christ, transforming the personality, bringing about birth or rebirth, recreating, overcoming the world, illuminating, bestowing the Spirit of God and bestowing the glory of God. This wealth of imagery illustrates the key fact of Christian experience. Sacrifice is only one image among a multitude of others.

Jesus certainly understood his coming death to have universal significance, as indeed it does. He speaks of giving his life as a ransom for many (Mark 10.45; Matthew 20.28), where 'for many' is a Hebraism meaning 'for all'. But this cannot have been intended to be taken literally, for to whom would the ransom have been paid? To his Heavenly Father, who accepted the death of Jesus as 'ransom money' for the release of the world's sins? This seems too crude a concept of God. If however we understand ransom as a metaphor, it has great value: it underlines the universal significance of Jesus's death, and emphasizes the costly self-giving of Jesus on the cross.

The Synoptic and the Pauline accounts of the institution of the Eucharist use language reminiscent not of ransom but of sacrifice. The cup of wine is 'my blood of the covenant poured out for many' (Mark 14.24). Is this reference to sacrificial blood really intended literally? (There was in fact the minimum of blood shed at a crucifixion.) If it was intended literally, then we need to ask, to whom was the sacrifice paid? To our Father in Heaven? If so, why? If the nature of God is love, it is hard to believe that the death of Jesus was the only way open to him to restore humankind's relationship to him.

It is true that sacrifice is one of the key categories in the rest of the New Testament (apart from the Epistle of St James), and that by it the death of Jesus is interpreted. It is for example the basic theme of the Epistle to the Hebrews. But that Epistle recognizes as a datum the efficacy of sacrifice, it is something axiomatic, and on this assumption its author has little difficulty in showing how the sacrificial death of Christ, our great high priest, fulfils all that the Old Testament sacrifices stood for but could not achieve. Paul also, as a good Jew, assumed the efficacy of sacrifice, and so too do the authors of I Peter and I John. Naturally they thought of Jesus's death as a efficacious sacrifice. Today, in our contemporary world, such an assumption has become very problematic, because we do not share the ancient world's belief in the efficacy of sacrifice in our relationship with the divine.

But if we understand sacrifice as a metaphor (like the reference to ransom), then we can appreciate that it was very appropriate imagery to have been used, in view of the multitude of sacrifices in the ancient world, both in the Jewish Temple and in pagan shrines. We use the metaphor of sacrifice today in a somewhat different sense, to signify not reconciliation and atonement, but costly self-giving service. Both sides in the last two Great Wars speak of the sacrifice of soldiers who died in these wars to indicate the costliness of their service to their country. When we speak of the sacrifice of Jesus, do we not mean that he gave himself up to death by a very costly act? He did it not in service to his country like soldiers in a war, but in utter loyalty to his Heavenly Father, and in fearless obedience to the truth, including his refusal to deny his special status and mission from God. By this costly act he suffered not only physical pain, but also the withdrawal of his Father's presence which brought him a sense of being utterly forsaken. In so doing he has helped millions of others; and his resurrection testifies to the spiritual power of that action. He teaches us that through self-sacrifice and the sense of forsakenness comes spiritual renewal and rebirth. When it is realized that this self-giving was made by one who is the perfect expression of God in terms of humanity, the death of Jesus is invested with a special significance. It almost brings tears to the eyes simply to contemplate it. No wonder the symbol of the cross has been so immensely powerful down the ages.

There have been many attempts to produce a doctrine of

atonement from images of transformation taken from the New Testament, such as sacrifice, ransom or justification. These images have been expanded into detailed doctrines. In feudal times there was a doctrinal theory based on the concept of satisfaction. In modern times a psychological model of the atonement has been advanced. All these theories attempt to explain the connection between the death of Christ and the radical spiritual change that he brings to believers. None of them are satisfactory. Perhaps the real reason why they do not succeed is because there is no need for such a doctrine.

It is certainly true that humankind is alienated from God. Although much good has been done by people, nonetheless the appalling record of man's terrible inhumanity to man, continued in every age, is sufficient witness to this awful truth; and even the Church cannot be exempted from this record. This alienation must be distinguished from sin. Sins are forgiven by God when we repent and purpose amendment, provided we act in a forgiving way towards others; while persistent refusal to accept or give love can lead us into a hell of our own making. Alienation is a different situation, one in which we find ourselves helpless. It used to be believed that it began with the fall of Adam, and a 'second Adam', as it were, was needed to remove the curse that hangs over humankind. It is certainly true that many people are alienated from God's love, or feel themselves alienated from him. But we no longer look back to a mythical Adam. Human beings are born self-centred, an inheritance they receive from their animal forebears and without which they could not survive in infancy. This self-centredness continues into adolescence and adulthood, and causes alienation from God. When it is combined with the need to generate feelings of self-worth it can lead to pride, and all the other deadly sins.

Some people seem to be born as it were naturally Christian – *anima naturaliter Christiana* – so that they do not appear to suffer alienation from God. For others God can break through this alienation in many ways. It is blessedly true that an encounter with God through the mediation of the risen Christ, whether gradual or sudden, can bring about a real transformation of character; and the wonderful record of Christian conversion down the ages attests this. Such an encounter can take many forms. One of these may not involve the death of Jesus at all; it may be simply the realization of Jesus's promise that 'where two or three are gathered together in my name, there am I in the midst of them' (Matthew 18.20). While for some this transcendental encounter may come through acceptance of the belief that 'Jesus died for me', for many this experience does not involve any particular interpretation of his death. The death of Christ was unique, not in the sense that it was a unique sacrifice, but because its guiltless victim was the One who perfectly expressed in terms of human personality the nature of God, and whom we therefore rightly regard as God Incarnate.

The radical transformation of those who have experienced the Transcendent, expressed in the many images used in the New Testament which I have detailed above, was brought about not just by this death, but by the whole 'event of Christ' including his life and above all his resurrection.

What was unique about Jesus Christ was the uniqueness of his person, as seen through his teaching, his ministry, his death and his resurrection. He gives us a personal expression of God in human terms; and from this we have unique insights into the nature of God, concerning his will, his love, his self-giving, his acceptingness, his Spirit. These insights are not merely illuminating: when they are believed in the depths of the soul, they effect a radical change of outlook in a believer.

Honesty however compels the admission that such transformation of character is to be found in other great world religions, such as Buddhism, Hinduism, Judaism and Islam. There is a plentiful record of saints in these religions who have had a transcendental encounter with the living God and whose lives have been transformed from self-centredness to self-giving. Is there therefore no difference between Christianity and these faiths? By no means. In the Christian faith we are given a personal disclosure of God's nature; that is to say, a revelation in a human person. Because we are human beings, a self-disclosure by God through a human being speaks more clearly to us and acts more powerfully upon us than any other kind of disclosure. Here Christ is unique. God spoke to Jews through the law and the prophets. Muhammad claimed only to be a prophet of God. The Buddha never claimed to be the divine self-disclosure of God. It is true that in the Indian tradition there have been *avatars*, allegedly incarnations of the godhead; but a comparison of the life and ministry of these with that of Jesus Christ shows them to be in a different category. There is salvation through other religions, but Christianity is unique because in it we are given the self-disclosure of God through the medium of human personality.

These words do not apply to each and every cult. 'Religion' is an umbrella term which can be used to describe wicked and satanic beliefs as well as those faiths inspired by God. There is a shadow side to religious faith, and many terrible evils have been done in the name of religion. One of the criteria which should be applied to a religion is to assess whether it leads to love, joy and peace not only among its own members but also among others.

Mainstream religions other than Christianity may well have some beliefs and practices which do not meet with the approval of Christians. At the same time non-Christian faiths, in the words of the Vatican Council, 'often reflect a ray of that Truth which enlightens all men' (*Nostra Aetate*, 2). We can go further than this. People have found in them a transforming awareness of the Transcendent which removes self-centredness, and they have experienced a moral claim on their conscience to do good to others.

There is indeed a global ethic shared by the great religions (Küng, 1993, p. 623), similar to Jesus's summary of the Old Testament law, that we must love God with all our heart and our neighbour as ourselves. This global ethic does not mean that all religions are the same; but it does show that they hold some basic truth in common.

The view being put forward here is both opposed to mere relativism (that all religions are the same), and it rejects a triumphant absolutism (that Christianity is the only true faith). 'The boundary between true and false today, even as Christians see it, no longer runs simply *between* Christianity and other religions, but at least in part *within* each of the religions. The principle here is that nothing of value in other religions is to be denied, but neither is anything of value to be uncritically accepted' (Küng, 1993, p. xix) . There will also be matters in their own faith which some Christians may not want to accept – in this chapter the traditional view of the atonement has been suggested as one of these – while at the same time there will be beliefs of other faiths which may shed new illumination on the Christian faith. And there are similarities. As I have gladly affirmed, non-Christians may be given an authentic awareness of God of such a kind that it transforms their lives from darkness to light, and from self-centredness to self-giving. No doubt we all, Christians and non-Christians, need further pilgrimage before we are judged worthy of the beatific vision. Christians rejoice that they have been given a *personal* revelation, and that through Christ they have been given a unique insight into spiritual realities. Without abandoning their convictions about this unique aspect of God's self-revelation in Jesus Christ, they should at the same time greet our brothers and sisters in other faiths as inheritors with us of the kingdom of God; and they should affirm them in their own right rather than as unconscious recipients of the grace of Christ. The Holy Spirit of God has been at work in them.

This by no means closes the door on Christian mission, but it does suggest a new paradigm of mission. Paradigm shifts have occurred before (Bosch, 1991). Mission must include disinterested service to those of other faiths. In matters of faith, mission must now begin with dialogue, as we explore each other's beliefs; and through dialogue it may (or it may not) lead to conversion to the Christian faith, with its personal, unique self-disclosure of God in terms of human personality.

7

The Nearly Last Things

We do not know what will happen to us when we die. We will only know when we die. Now that I am an octogenarian, that knowledge cannot be long delayed so far as I am concerned! But while we live on earth as human beings, our future destiny is hidden from us, except in the most general terms. Will we exist at all? If so, will we have the same kind of prejudices, fears, and failings as when we were alive? What will it be like to live outside space and time (if 'outside' is the right term)? How can we exist apart from our present bodies of flesh and blood? As a Western man, I feel also inclined to ask: 'What shall we *do*?'

We should not be surprised at this lack of knowledge. We are surrounded by mystery in this life. There are many things that are mysterious in the natural sciences. Our senses only record a small range of what is going on around us, because the process of evolution has only caused us to develop knowledge necessary for our development and survival. Similarly we only have a small range of spiritual knowledge. It is better to profess ignorance rather than to pretend to certainty about what we do not know.

It is clear (at least to me) that the Scriptures speak only in terms of symbol and imagery. How can we sit down to a feast in the kingdom of God if we will have no teeth or taste-buds or stomach? How can we play on harps without hands to finger the strings? Furthermore, the imagery used in the New Testament is largely that which was current in the contemporary Jewish world of the time of Jesus and the early Church. It is none the worse for that; but it is not the imagery of our contemporary world. It was then generally believed that God would in a flash transform the world. He hasn't. From what the scientists tell us, the universe is likely to go on expanding until there is a heat death; and long before that the sun will increase in size until it swallows up Planet Earth, if it hasn't been knocked out by a large meteor or comet before that. Christians believed that Christ's return to earth was imminent, but it wasn't. It seems that Jesus himself believed that too. (That was natural, if he thought of himself as God's special agent, and shared in the belief that the end of the world was imminent.) It was commonly believed that there would be a general resurrection of the dead, which St Paul thought at one time would come in his own lifetime. It didn't. There are of course important spiritual truths behind all these beliefs. Images of heaven implied that it would be a sphere of joy and fulfilment. Images of the end of the world implied that God has a purpose and plan for his creation which will finally be fulfilled. The imagery of new spiritual bodies implied that after death there is a fresh mode of personal existence. The truths are vital: the imagery in which they were expressed is not.

Those who find this unsettling would do well to meditate on the fundamentals of our Christian faith, validated by experience. The first is that Jesus is alive, that he rose from the dead on the third day, and that he is the first-fruits of them that sleep. In other words Christ has demonstrated that death is not the end, but only the end of the beginning. A second foundation stone is the belief of Christians, again validated in experience, that God is love and we are created to share in his love, so that whatever happens to us after death will be the expression of God's continuing love for each one of us.

The Western Church developed concepts of heaven, hell and purgatory. Heaven is our final destiny, a state (one cannot call it a place) of joy unimaginable, the realization of the beatific vision, living in the very presence of God whose nature is perfect love, where all our fears and blindnesses, our shortcomings and selfishness have been shed, where we are free to live in mutual love, blessed peace and perfect communion with the Eternal God and in fellowship with our fellows. Some mystics claim to have lived in this state, but for most of us we have only had a fragmentary glimpse of what it might be like. It is so unlike our present state that it can only be described in terms of negatives or by the use of human analogies. Physical union and married bliss are perhaps the metaphors most used by the mystics to describe it. A lesser mortal (Sydney Smith) has described it as 'eating pâté de foie gras to the sound of trumpets'.

Hell is the very opposite. It used to be thought to be where unbelievers went. It was believed to be a place of eternal torment and punishment for mortal sins. Fortunately our ideas have moved on. Few people think of it in these terms today. Nowadays hell is the destiny of those – if there be any – who eternally refuse to respond to love, unless indeed they be decreated (annihilated). To be unable to relate to people as God intends us to do, to be unable to give or receive love; this must be an appalling eternal deprivation if any are in that state. God is love, and so he deals lovingly with every soul, and because no one can love to order, he gives us freedom to deny our nature (permanently, if we so will) and to refuse to accept or to give love.

Fundamentalist Christians hold that when we die, we sleep until the Last Judgement after which we are raised up to heaven 'at the last day' with new spiritual bodies (or sent down to hell). Others hold that, apart perhaps for great saints, the rest of us who aspire to heaven need further training to be fit for this immense inheritance. Purgatory used to be thought by Roman Catholics to be a sphere where expiation is made after death for venial sins and where punishment is administered for mortal sins that have already been forgiven. Indulgences – that is, the remission of so many 'days' of punishment in purgatory – are still sometimes offered in the Roman Catholic Church as a reward for good works. However in the recent English *Catechism of the Catholic Church* the concepts of purgatorial punishment (rejected in the

Church of England in its Articles of Religion) are soft-pedalled.
Instead we have:

> All who die in God's grace and friendship, but still imperfectly
> purified, are indeed assured of their eternal salvation; but after
> death they undergo purification, so as to achieve the holiness
> necessary to enter the Kingdom of Heaven. (*Catechism*, p.
> 235)

Personally I prefer the Eastern Orthodox concept of *theosis* or
divinization where we receive training to make us less immature
and more godlike so that, to use traditional language, we may
progress from being made in the image of God to be made into
the likeness of God: in other words, we undergo not simply
purification from earlier bad habits and attitudes but
sanctification and hallowing so that we will be able to respond
more fully to the nearer presence of the eternal God.

Is it possible that as a preamble to entering it, God sends some
souls back to earth reincarnated in different personalities so that they
may make more progress here on earth towards the goal of heaven,
or, for the more advanced souls, so that they may assist others making
their earthly pilgrimage? Belief in reincarnation is held by many
millions of people who belong to Eastern religions. A belief so
strongly held by so many should not be cast aside without proper
investigation. The question of reincarnation is so underinvestigated
that the rest of this chapter will be concerned with it.

It is popularly thought that the Christian Church has rejected
reincarnation. This is not precisely the case. It certainly has not
been endorsed, but I can find no anathema of a General Council
against it. I consulted Professor Henry Chadwick, a polymath in
these matters, who responds: 'There is no decree of an
ecumenical council known to me which explicitly outlaws belief
in the transmigration of souls.' He warns me however that
'censures and anathemas by ecumenical councils are not
necessary to define the limits of credenda'. Nonetheless the fact

that reincarnation has not been formally condemned permits a serious consideration of the matter, in the belief that Christian thinkers should always be open to new insights into truth.

If reincarnation were ever to be considered seriously as a Christian doctrine, it would have to be distinguished in certain particulars from the beliefs held about it in Eastern religions. There it is associated with *karma*, so that one's state of being in the next life is dependent on one's behaviour in this one. Again some Eastern religions hold that if one has a bad *karma*, this may make one regress to some subhuman species hereafter; whereas a Christian view of reincarnation would hold that people might return to earth in a different human personality to assist the soul (or other souls) in growth into holiness. (For all we know, persons might be reincarnated in planets unknown to us elsewhere in our universe, or in other universes where life is different from our carbon-based existence.) Furthermore, Eastern religions hold that *everyone* is subject to reincarnation, which recurs again and again until a person gains liberation and reaches *nirvana*, whereas a Christian view would be that reincarnation need apply only to certain persons, with a limited number of reincarnations, either because they could gain spiritually by such a process or because they would help others in the earthly pilgrimage. While the Eastern doctrines hold a pessimistic view of this world, the Christian religion is positive, believing that the created world is essentially good and regarding it as a place of soul-making.

Christian objections to reincarnation could be various. One might be that at death Christians are given an immediate vision of God as he is in himself. Paul wrote that he would rather depart and be with Christ (Philippians 1.23) but he usually speaks of the dead not as though they were in heaven but rather as those who sleep in Christ. Jesus's words to the penitent thief on the cross, as recorded by St Luke, were: 'This day you will be with me in Paradise' (Luke 23.43), but the Greek word *paradisos*, transliterated here as Paradise, means a garden, which suggests some future sphere which is not yet heaven itself. (In near-death experiences, it is not uncommon for people to find themselves in a garden.) Then there are those who hold that fundamental decisions concerning our future destiny are irrevocably made in this present life. If so, why are we told in the Scriptures that Christ, after his death, preached to the disobedient spirits in prison (1 Peter 3.19)? Others object that, according to Paul, we are promised when we die not another earthly body but a spiritual body (1 Corinthians 15.44). This is so. Paul did not himself accept reincarnation, but the point he was making is that after death we do not exist as bare souls, but as psychophysical entities, and this is certainly consonant with reincarnation.

If Paul did not believe in reincarnation, can it be found elsewhere in the New Testament? According to St Mark's Gospel, followed by St Matthew's Gospel, when Jesus came down from the mountain after his transfiguration, his disciples asked him why the scribes taught that Elijah must come first (in accordance with the prophecy in Malachi). Jesus is said to have replied: 'Yes, Elijah does come first, to set everything right...I tell you that Elijah has already come, and they have worked their will upon him, as the Scriptures say of him' (Mark. 9.12–13; Matthew 17.11–12). This is clearly an identification of Elijah with John the Baptist. Commentators have understood the verse to mean that John carried out the prophetic role of Elijah. But that is not what Jesus is reported to have said. He said Elijah had already come. Elijah did not descend from heaven in the time of Jesus in a way similar to the biblical account of his disappearance from the earth. We know who were John's father and mother, and although he had elderly parents, he was born in the normal way. Clearly John was a different person from Elijah, shaped by different cultures and different environments, although their characters were to some degree identical. The simplest explanation of Jesus's sayings is that Elijah was reincarnated in John the Baptist.

This was not the only occasion when John was identified with Elijah. Jesus is reported to have said: 'All the prophets and the law prophesied until John, and if you are willing to receive it, he is Elijah who is to come' (Matthew 11.13). Again, it is difficult to interpret this verse other than by regarding John as Elijah reincarnated. Other people too made the same identification (Mark 6.15; 9.8). The very first question that the priestly delegation asked Jesus when they came from Jerusalem was, according to St John's Gospel: 'Are you Elijah?' (John 1.21). Others too thought he was Elijah (Mark 6.15), while others held he was another of the prophets (Mark 6.16). When Jesus on another occasion asked his disciples whom people thought that he was, he was told that people believed he was Elijah or John the Baptist or one of the prophets (Mark 8.28). Elsewhere these prophets are identified as Elijah or Jeremiah (Matthew 16.14) or one of the other prophets (Luke 9.19). While I recognize that it is possible to interpret these Gospel passages as referring to the belief that the spirit of Elijah or one of the prophets rested on Jesus, this seems a forced interpretation in view of the fact that it was believed that the Spirit of God descended on Jesus at his baptism. Reincarnation cannot be ruled out as giving the correct interpretation.

There is a positive advantage to belief in reincarnation. Christians have never come to terms with problems concerning the future destiny of those who die in infancy or early childhood. An infant's brain is not yet fully formed. The character is not yet fully set. The infant has had no chance to mature into a fully formed human person. What is the future destiny of such an unformed personality after death? In Latin theology the *limbo* is the abode of souls, still suffering from original sin and excluded from the full blessedness of the beatific vision, but not condemned to any punishment. This was said to be the abode of unbaptized infants, held to be excluded from supernatural beatitude. St Thomas Aquinas believed that they attain full natural happiness. This concept of the *limbo* is unacceptable today. But the question remains: what does happen to infants and young children who die? How can they make full relationships with others and with God? They have not yet developed sufficiently to do this. It would seem in accordance with natural justice that they should be reincarnated in another body and have the opportunity of maturing as adults towards full spiritual as well as physical development. It is interesting that 51 per cent of young children claiming to have lived former lives assert that they died by violence when young.

I do not pretend that the notion of reincarnation is without difficulty. Does reincarnation, if it happens, take place immediately? It would seem from evidence of mediums, if this can be believed, that our present personality persists for a time after death and before reincarnation. We may distinguish the soul, the inner spiritual core of existence which bears the essence of a person's character, from the psyche, which is conditioned by contemporary culture and predilections and prejudices. It would be the soul and not the psyche which is reincarnated. While a person matures as much from nurture and environment as from nature and inheritance, nonetheless we know that genetic inheritance does incline a person towards certain attitudes and characteristics. It is obvious that the fitting of a soul to an inheritance different from that of its former life would not be the easiest of tasks! I leave on one side how reincarnation could come about, and how the right choice of a new embryo could be made – for presumably the choice would have to be made from the time of conception. Who would make it or how it would be made, I have no idea; but it is not logically impossible. Furthermore, we do not know whether memories of a former life would have simply been repressed, so that finally the soul has to review them and come to terms with earlier behaviour. On the other hand it might well be that memories have been blotted out, since it is only the soul, and not the psyche, that is carried into a further existence.

So difficult is the idea of reincarnation for a Westerner to accept that there would have to be very good evidence indeed in favour of it before a reasonable person could find himself convinced. Does such evidence exist?

Many people have the feeling of déjà vu when they feel that they have been in a place before, although they know that they have not in their present existence. However, this is a trick played on us by our brain, and we need not take it seriously. Again, I have known people who have found themselves addicted to some past or far distant culture, such as that of ancient Greece or, more contemporarily, of India. Why do they have this addiction? Is it because of a past reincarnation? The evidence is too thin to be taken seriously.

Again people have had dreams in which they exist in a different personality. At the time the dream, like all dreams, is self-authenticating. When we awake we usually regard them as fictions made up by the unconscious mind. Of course dreams suggesting a previous existence *might* be genuine insights into a past life, but, when measured against other dreams, it seems exceedingly unlikely that this would be the case. Further, there are adults who claim to remember their past lives. A well-known example is Dr Arthur Guirdham who claims to remember details of his previous existence as a Cathar. But we human beings are very prone to fantasizing.

More convincing at first sight are those who produce detailed evidence of a past life under hypnosis. Once again, these might possibly be authentic memories, but when one considers the nature of hypnosis, it seems very unlikely. A person who is hypnotized automatically obeys the wishes of the hypnotist. 'Tell me about your past lives,' the hypnotist may say, and the person hypnotized has to oblige. If there is no such memory, the person is bound to make one up. Some remarkable past lives have been recorded under hypnosis. A well-known instance is that of Virginia Tighe who remembered a previous life in Ireland.

Among the 'Bloxham Tapes' there are the recollections of Jane Evans, a woman who alleged that in the past she was tutor to Constantine when he was a boy while his family was living in England; and later a maid to Catherine of Aragon, and four other lives. Some intelligent researcher found that there exist historical romances with characters of the same names as Jane Evans alleged she remembered. Much, perhaps all, we have said or read is stored in the unconscious mind, and no doubt the woman had read these books, and had even forgotten that she had read them, and the unconscious mind dredged them up and used them in obeying the hypnotist's request for details of past lives.

None of these sources provides reliable evidence for a belief in reincarnation.

However there is another fruitful source which has been carefully investigated over many years by a serious and scholarly researcher. Children between the ages of two and eight can produce remarkably accurate accounts of their alleged former lives. Admittedly this happens mostly in cultures where reincarnation is taken for granted; but not entirely so. In any case children in cultures where reincarnation is rejected and who do allege knowledge of earlier lives are unlikely to be believed. No doubt their parents dismiss this as childish talk and tell them to stop talking nonsense; and so they do stop. After eight years of age the memory of a former existence seems to fade: occasionally it may last until the eleventh year. (Perhaps it is merely suppressed.) The memories of a previous life are both cognitive and behavioural; that is to say, they are not only concerned with people and places, but also they affect behaviour.

Professor Ian Stevenson of the University of Virginia is the person who has pioneered this research. He has investigated with scholarly thoroughness over 2,600 such children, and published 65 detailed reports. He has interviewed children in India, Burma, Thailand, Sri Lanka, Turkey, the Lebanon, and among the Tlingit peoples of Alaska and the Ibos of Nigeria, as well as some in the Western world. He has helpers in different countries who spot from papers or hearsay children who allege knowledge of former lives, as it is necessary to interview them as soon as may be, if possible before they have visited the families where they allege they have belonged. Professor Stevenson guards against such persons' prejudices in favour of reincarnation. His case histories include the persons interviewed who have heard the child's claims, the relevant geography and the possibility of communication between the two families concerned, the attitudes of the parents, statements about their recognitions of places and people of an alleged former existence, and the verification of the contents of what is claimed.

It has been alleged that children may fraudulently assert they have formerly lived earlier lives in better conditions, in order to boost their ego or to escape from the lowly status of their present lives; but investigation has shown that children may claim that they had a lower status in a previous life. Furthermore, their claim, far from magnifying their status, can be a matter of embarrassment to their parents. All this has to be investigated before a judgement can be made in any particular case.

It would not be appropriate in this short chapter to give detailed examples of claims to previous lives. These can be found in the many case histories that Professor Stevenson has recorded and published. But what is to be made of a young child who insists he is married and has two sons, and speaks of their names and where they live, and recognizes them after he has made such a fuss that his parents at length take him to the place where they live? What is to be made of a child who shows a phobia relating to the violent death he alleges he suffered in an earlier life, and after investigation of hospital records, etc. it is found that the person he alleges he was in a former existence did die a violent death exactly as he said? There is the possibility when past lives are said to be remembered that the person concerned is in telepathic communication with someone else, and derives details of past lives from this source. But it is difficult to maintain this when a child shows no sign of any psychic gifts, and yet can even remember some mark in a house he made in his (alleged) earlier life which the previous family did not know about until he pointed it out. What is to be made of children who dislike the food that is set before them, and hanker after food to which they say they were accustomed in an earlier existence and which turns out to be the food usually eaten in the district where they allege they had lived?

Professor Stevenson has produced even more extraordinary evidence in favour of reincarnation. He has found birthmarks and birth defects which appear to be the result of events in an earlier life. The odds against this happening by chance are very large. Professor Stevenson has published a large and extensive multi-volume medical monograph, with extensive documentation, references, numerous tables and many footnotes, giving details of this (Stevenson, 1997a). In a shorter work he has provided summaries of 112 cases out of the 225 examined in the larger book, together with photographs of the more striking examples (Stevenson, 1997b). For example, a boy who claimed to have been shot dead in an earlier existence was found to have birthmarks in the throat (where the shot entered) and a larger birthmark in the head (where the shot exited); wounds verified in post-mortems and medical reports. These birthmarks tend to move and then fade as the child grows older, in the same kind of way as cognitive and behavioural memories fade. It seems that, if reincarnation is a reality, we are not intended to know about our earlier existence, but the memory which affects the soul has been imperfectly repressed in early days, although after a few years the fault is rectified and the memory disappears.

In addition to birthmarks, Stevenson claims that birth defects may be passed on to a reincarnated existence. In his shorter work he gives 15 examples of the far larger number examined in the large monograph. He notes three kinds of defects: birth defects which occur in the extremities of the body, those which occur in the neck or head, and those which occur in two or more areas of the body. The correspondences, carefully and painstakingly researched, match exactly those of an alleged former existence: they are extraordinary.

Birthmarks and birth defects are important evidence, for the odds against their random occurrence is very high, and they cannot be explained as the product of telepathic communication or childish fraud. It seems as though the union of body and soul is so close that it can affect a future body of a reincarnated soul. Be this as it may, the work of Professor Stevenson cannot give decisive proof of reincarnation; but his scientific methodology and his extraordinary findings deserve wider recognition, especially among those opposed to the idea of reincarnation. They should be taken seriously.

It seems that reincarnation is both compatible with the Christian faith, and also supported by excellent if not conclusive evidence. However the matter must be seen in proper perspective. Whatever happens to us after death, we are being prepared for the final goal of our existence. If reincarnation does take place, it is only one further stage on the pilgrimage of human beings en route for our final destiny. It is not the end for which we have been created, which is to enjoy the beatific vision in loving union with God for all eternity. It is that goal which is all important.

8

Belief in God

Why do people believe? There are many answers to such a question, some more respectable than others. A better question is: 'What are the grounds of belief?' How well founded is theism? Just how strong are the arguments for God's existence?

One evening at a dinner party in the 1830s a French atheist was affirming his conviction that there is no God. Sydney Smith, present at the dinner table, turned to him and said, 'Did you enjoy your soufflé?' The Frenchman, being a Frenchman, took the question seriously and replied, 'Yes, very much'. 'Do you doubt', Smith riposted, 'the existence of the cook?' Evidently Sydney Smith had been convinced by the kind of arguments that Archdeacon Paley deployed with his famous parable of a watch found in the middle of a road providing evidence of its maker. Nowadays this type of argument rings few bells (except perhaps in fundamentalist circles), because the theory of natural selection through random mutation seems to negate it. Hence the title of Richard Dawkins' book, *The Blind Watchmaker* (1986).

However, another argument from design for the existence of God has developed during the last century, of a different type. Some fifteen years ago I outlined this new way of thinking in a book called *The Probability of God* (Montefiore, 1985). A series of apparently amazing coincidences in the constants of fundamental forces had been discovered – I listed 11 and since then more have been described – ranging from the distribution of gases in the early universe to the mass of the universe, from the relative weight of neutrons, protons and electrons to the process by which in the centre of hot stars carbon is formed which is scattered abroad when a supernova explodes and which forms the basis of all living systems. Even a minute difference in distribution or weight or process would have meant that there would be no galaxies, no stars could form, or the universe would have collapsed on itself, or there would be no carbon-based life.

Has the situation altered since then? I believe that the 'strong anthropic argument' has grown stronger. It does appear extraordinary that, seemingly against all the odds, galaxies, stars and planets such as our own have formed and that on this planet life has emerged and developed into *Homo sapiens*. In order for this to happen, the initial conditions of the universe had to be precisely just so. If we are not unique, and if there are other universes like ours, their initial conditions must be identical with our own. What are the odds against this happening? Roger Penrose, Rouse Ball professor of mathematics in Oxford, calculated them. He put them at $10^{10^{123}}$. 'If I were to put one zero on each elementary particle in the Universe', he has written, 'I still could not put the number down in full. It is a stupendous number' (Penrose *et al.*, 1997, p. 48). Since carbon-based life is the only form of which we have any knowledge, this forces us to ask afresh whether our universe could possibly have come into being by mere chance rather than by design.

The answer is, 'Yes, it could'. All these apparent coincidences could have happened by mere chance. But this would involve one of three possibilities. Perhaps there are an infinite number of universes. If so, it would seem inevitable that one at least would turn out to have precisely the same characteristics as our own universe, however long the odds are against this. Or our universe may be only one domain of an infinite or hugely vast 'multiverse'. The same then would apply. Or, it has been held, every time a new observation is made, and the quantum wave collapses, a new world comes into being, resulting in an unimaginably vast multiplicity of worlds in which one like our own is bound to come into being. The problem of all these three possibilities is that there is absolutely no evidence to show that any of them is true. They are subject to the law of Occam's Razor – if a simpler explanation will do, we should use it. But they remain possibilities, however seemingly remote. The fact that there is this strange set of coincidences among the constants of nature's basic forces has certainly helped to strengthen my own faith; but it only *proves* that these coincidences are necessary for the emergence of our world: it does not prove that there is necessarily a design to the universe.

Similar results apply to a consideration of Planet Earth. Take for example the atmosphere which surrounds it. Without this, cosmic rays from the sun would preclude the possibility of life on the earth. It has lately been discovered (or perhaps 'inferred' would be the right word) that there are many more planets among the billions of the stars belonging to the billions of galaxies in the universe. Since the atmosphere of the earth has developed from a hydrogen type atmosphere to its present mix (Lovelock, 1979, p. 18), it seems very improbable that, if there are atmospheres surrounding other planets, they would be similar to that which surrounds the earth today. Improbable, yes; but still possible. The existence of our kind of atmosphere in no way *proves* that it is the product of design.

Again, in the 1998 Leonard Award Lecture (Taylor, 1999, pp. 317–29) the difficulties of earth-like planets being formed elsewhere in the universe are discussed. The lecturer pointed out that rocky planets owe their particular composition to the operation of a random accumulation process. Since the process is random, the existence of tectonic plates which form the platform above which the later stages of our planet's evolution took place is probably unique, as is the presence of the continental crust which has developed through plate tectonics. I am not versed in geology, and so I cannot discuss the technicalities, but the argument mounted by Professor Taylor is deeply impressive. On the other hand, the fact that our earth has a continental crust and tectonic plates, with the probability that this is unique, in no way *proves* that it is the product of design.

In *The Probability of God* I took up Dr James Lovelock's 'Gaia hypothesis' (Lovelock, 1979) that the biosphere has developed its own feedback mechanisms which (unless grossly interfered with by human beings) keep the planet comfortable for life, and I adduced this as a further example for design in the universe. Dr Lovelock has shown that organic life as well as inorganic substances contribute to the stability of the biosphere, and that the evolution of organisms must take into account the evolution of the environment. So far as the atmosphere is concerned, this has resulted in a small (but necessary) amount of methane in the atmosphere, while oxygen is a consistent 21 per cent of its contents (which is optimum for life); and so far as the oceans are concerned, the saltiness of the sea is consistent at 3.4 per cent (disastrous results would ensue if it rose to 6 per cent).

In the 1980s the Gaia hypothesis was regarded as 'way out' by most of Dr Lovelock's fellow scientists. This was perhaps partly due to adoption of the phrase by 'New Agers' in a way that its author never intended, but more probably because it cut across assumptions which scientists hold dear, for it necessitates modification of the Darwinian theory of evolution. In the history of science there are many examples of theories now taken for granted which were originally rejected on this account (e.g., the existence of tectonic plates).

Gaia theory certainly had its critics. Dawkins, the great evangelist of neo-Darwinism, used scathingly to dismiss it because it stressed co-operation in nature rather than survival of the fittest. Lovelock illustrated his theory by his 'Daisyworld' parable of a planet with only white and black daisies which by this means maintained a stable temperature. Opposition to the hypothesis is understandable, for, as Lovelock wrote: 'If Daisyworld is valid, then seventy-five years of neo-Darwinist science will need to be rewritten.' Lovelock strengthened his theory by showing how climate is affected over the oceans through the emission of dimethyl sulphide from algae in the water, which makes possible the formation of rain drops over the sea. To quote Lovelock once again, 'the theory of a self-regulating Earth, able to maintain climate and chemistry always tolerable for its existence, is now moving into acceptance as part of scientific wisdom'. Twenty years on, the Gaia hypothesis has become respectable.

I argued in *The Probability of God* that this theory further lengthens the odds against Planet Earth being the product of pure randomness and that it made it more likely to be the product of design. I am sure that this is the case for those who already believe in God, and it has certainly helped to strengthen my own faith. But on further reflection I think that I ought to have paid more attention to the fact that the author of the theory himself is what may be called a 'benevolent agnostic'. If it doesn't make him believe in the existence of God, why should it do this to anyone else, until there is already existing belief? Extraordinary coincidences do occur, however improbable or even impossible they may seem before they happen, as many can testify in their own lives, when, say, in a remote part of the world one suddenly meets a friend or an acquaintance.

The same must be said about the emergence of life on earth. It is so improbable that it has been seriously argued that life arrived on the planet from some source outside it, although such a suggestion in no way explains how it originated. Francis Crick wrote: 'An honest man, armed with all the knowledge available to us now, could only state that in some sense, the origin of life appears at the moment to be almost a miracle, so many are the conditions which would have had to be satisfied to get it going' (Crick, 1981, p. 88). But Crick himself is a (fairly militant) atheist, as well as being a very intelligent person who discovered the 'double helix' of DNA which provides the ground plan of human life. Once again, to the believer the emergence of life seems too improbable to have occurred by mere chance and thus it provides evidence of a Creator; but it certainly does not have this effect on an unbeliever.

How did the cell evolve? We do not know. It is, after all, very complex. The earliest forms of life known to us, the procariotes, have been dated three-and-a-half billion years ago. It took a couple of billion years for these to evolve into eukariotes, with their molecular apparatus for generating and controlling movement within the cell. How all this happened we do not know. Many people assume that natural selection by random mutation explains the whole panorama of evolution from that point to the present day. Apart from fundamentalists, most people in the West accept that we human beings have developed and evolved from these primitive forms of life; but just how that happened is a matter which is hotly debated. Darwinism is generally accepted, but neo-Darwinism, with its dogmatic assertion that natural selection through random mutation is the *only* means by which life evolved, is certainly not. There are many things that cannot be explained in this way. This is not of course to say that they may never be explained by Darwinian theory, but it does leave open the possibility of some other explanation. In any case the Darwinian theology of evolution needs to be modified if the Gaia hypothesis is accepted.

There have not been any great advances in evolutionary knowledge in the last 15 years. Stephen Jay Gould has shown from fossil evidence in the Burgess Shale that evolution was not a straight line but that early forms of life took some very strange and diverse shapes which did not survive; and he has claimed that the tendency towards complexity began with simple forms of life because increasing complexity was the result of the only available genetic mutation (Gould, 1989).

Atheists often claim that neo-Darwinism leaves no room for a Creator. Darwin's agnosticism was certainly confirmed by his theory of evolution. But the evidence is ambiguous, and may be used in favour of a Creator. For believers claim that although the Creator did not plan the course of evolution or intervene as it progressed, he did create the conditions which made evolution inevitable, and he would have known the kind of outcome that would ensue. For such people evolution confirms their belief in God rather than negates it.

There remains to be considered the nature of human beings. Do these suggest or prove the existence of a Creator? Evidently they are to be distinguished from other living beings, even though they share more than 95 per cent of their genes with chimpanzees. The higher mammals have some intelligence and rudimentary powers of thought, and even the humble bee has a memory. But human beings can express their thoughts in speech, they have developed superior powers of thought, imagination and appreciation, and they can introduce moral, aesthetic and even spiritual criteria into their thinking and activities. There are those who regard these faculties merely as extrapolations from animal endowments, while others regard them as in some respects reflecting divine attributes, so that they are said to be made 'in the image of God'. Again, there is ambiguity.

The morality of men and women can be evaluated in very different ways, as derived from the righteousness of God, or in purely secular terms, with altruism explained as the unconscious action of the 'selfish gene' which countenances self-sacrifice in order to boost a similar one found in near relatives (not that this accounts for the morality of the Good Samaritan). Human love, which many find the highest of all human experiences and a reflection in human beings of the love of God, is regarded by others as a refinement of animal lust and as a mere extension of bonding among mammals and birds to promote reproduction and nurture. As for beauty, for many it simply lies in the eye of the beholder, provoking the remark 'I know what I like.' Even those who admit there is an objectivity in beauty, composed of harmony, balance, proportion and light, do not necessarily regard it as a reflection of the beauty of God. Similarly, human creativity, seen by some as mirroring the creativity of God, is by others regarded merely as the product of the developed human brain.

What of religious experience? Research has found that this is widespread, which is perhaps surprising, for in the UK people do not easily speak of such matters. If people do experience the immanence of God within their hearts, they may put this down simply to their subjective psychological feelings. An experience, of divine transcendence is likely to make a deeper and more lasting impression. But with the passage of time such religious experience may lose its force. It is not necessary to the commitment of faith. I have known deeply committed Christians who have maintained that they have never had any religious experience whatsoever in their lives. Furthermore, to the religious person many experiences are regarded as religious, but an unreligious person, with the exactly same kind of experience, does not regard it as religious. It depends how it is interpreted. For those believers who do have it, it is self-authenticating, and provides for them direct proof of God's existence. How can they possibly experience a direct relationship with God unless they believe in him? But those who do not have any religious experience do not see it in this light. They regard it as the result of a particular kind of activity in the human cortex, which may be stimulated by electrodes, or as a psychological quirk resulting from cultural upbringing. Religious experience is ambiguous. Obviously it does make a difference, but the absence of it cannot be regarded as the deciding factor for the growth of unbelief in Western Europe.

So far as scientific knowledge of the cosmos, the galaxies, the stars and Planet Earth are concerned, the facts now known seem (to me) to point strongly towards design, and therefore towards God, while our knowledge of the evolution of species and of the characteristics of humanity, although consonant with the existence of the Creator, is ambiguous. Whereas believers often want to ask the question Why, others are content to accept things as they are without enquiring why they are as they are. For example, believers ask why anything exists at all, believing that only God provides a satisfactory answer to the question, whereas others are content to accept that things do exist, without wanting to enquire into their origin or possible purpose.

A case in point is the origin of the universe. It is now fairly universally agreed among scientists that the universe began from a singularity. There are those who explain this as due to the creative action of God. Others however believe that, since a vacuum contains virtual entities which pass very swiftly in and out of existence, one particular such entity in the vacuum which existed when the universe had not yet come into being, inflated into our primordial universe. While a theist would want to ask why a vacuum is full of such virtual entities, others are not interested. They just accept that it is.

There are some who think that our universe may be only one part of a very large or infinite 'multiverse'. There can of course be no proof of this. The Astronomer Royal admits that such a hypothesis flouts Occam's Razor, but he has suggested a way in which it might one day be tested (Rees, 2002, pp. 165, 175–8). In an infinite number of universes, at least one such as our own would be bound to turn up, which would explain the extraordinary 'coincidences' by which the fundamental laws have made possible life on our planet, while minute mathematical changes in these laws would make it impossible. But this is not an argument either for or against ascribing it to the creativity of God. God could have created a multiverse, or this might just be the way things are.

Again, it is a remarkable fact that the universe is comprehensible to the human mind, and it is generally assumed (and indeed forms the assumption behind all scientific research) that the way things are can always be logically explained. Theists suppose that this is because the created world is the work of an all-wise Creator; but others accept the rationality of the universe because this is the way it is. Theists want to ask the question, 'Why': others regard that as an illegitimate question.

I have spent much time looking at the reasons which may be given for the existence of God, because they are important. But none of them is conclusive, and, while I personally find that they assist my faith, I have to admit that far from bringing others to faith, they often seem to have no effect on them at all. Although arguments from nature increase the probability that there is design in the universe, most people do not subject the natural world to this kind of reasoning, and many perhaps would not grasp its significance. It is extraordinary that, although there is a spiritual searching in a time of spiritual vacuum, there is an increasing amount of agnosticism and unbelief at the very period when arguments derived from science have greatly increased the probability of God's existence. But we need to remember that arguments from the natural world can tell us nothing about the nature of God, only about the probability of his existence. This may well be the main reason why they are regarded as irrelevant by many people.

The environment in which a person is raised, or in which his or her life is lived, influences (but does not determine) whether a person is likely to be a believer or a unbeliever. In a purely secular society in which no mention is made of God, it seems unlikely that many will be brought to faith. But it does happen: the extraordinary revival of Christianity in post-Marxist Russia is a case in point. On the other hand in a culture where Christianity is generally accepted, it seems unlikely that unbelief will grow. But once again, it does happen. The Victorian era is generally thought to have been particularly religious, yet there were many eminent unbelievers, as Owen Chadwick pointed out in his *Victorian Church* (vol. ii, 1972, pp. 112ff.) and A. N. Wilson has dramatically described in *God's Funeral* (1999). The culture of family life in which children are brought up is likely to affect their religious commitment. On the other hand it is well known that children can react against such a family culture: vicarage children often do. The 1960s was a period of student rebellion and reaction, and many then turned their back on their parents' beliefs; but their children who are students today have hardly reacted against *their* parents' unbelief. We must look deeper for the present religious malaise in Western Europe.

A further possible explanation for declining religious commitment could be that so many people now live in cities. They inhabit an almost entirely humanly-made world. In the secular city they live in a concrete jungle. They hardly ever see the world of nature. As a result of street lighting the night sky is never really dark, and as a result the multitude of stars is seldom seen. There is little opportunity to observe the rhythm of the seasons in the countryside, except perhaps on holiday; but even this is problematic as so many people head for the built-up environment of foreign seaside resorts. This probably contributes to unbelief, but it is difficult to accept that it is the chief explanation.

What then is the main reason for disbelief, which is so common today? I think it is probably the existence of evil, pain, suffering and natural disasters. People find it difficult to believe in a loving God when there is so much suffering and evil. To give an egregious example, it is usually thought that Darwin turned into an agnostic because of the negative effect on him of his work on evolution and the survival of the fittest. Certainly this did have an effect on him, but it was not conclusive. It was the early death of his beloved daughter Annie in 1851 which was the culminating moment:

> Annie had not deserved to die, she had not even deserved to be punished – in this world, let alone the next. 'Formed to live a life of happiness', as Charles put it, she had stumbled on ill health and nature's check fell upon her, crushing her

remorselessly. The struggle was 'bitter and cruel' enough without the prospect of retribution. Yet against the odds, he still longed that she might survive. He was haunted by her face, her loving kisses and her tears... Annie's cruel death destroyed Charles's tatters of belief in a moral, just universe. Later he would say that this period chimed the final death-knell for his Christianity, even if it had been a long drawn out process of decay. (Desmond and Moore, 1992, p. 387)

It is these personal crises that so often determine a person's deepest beliefs. And there are comparatively few people who have not met disaster, catastrophe, injustice and tragedy somewhere either in their own lives or among their loved ones, whether these be friends or family. This is compounded by those disasters in which thousands and tens of thousands die, or (as in the Holocaust) where the number runs into millions. There is widespread horror at the evil that people can do to one another, and the recent mass killings, in Africa and the Balkans and elsewhere, increase the sense of outrage. People are appalled by natural catastrophes, like the recent earthquake in Gujarat in India, or the tragedies wrought by tropical storms and tsunamis. People say to themselves: can there be a God if he allows such things to happen? How can he be a God of love, even assuming that human love is only a metaphor through which we try to picture God's love?

This is a potent reason for unbelief; but even here not all people react to disaster and distress in this kind of way. For example there is the outstanding case of Gordon Wilson, the man whose daughter was killed by IRA terrorists who forgave the murderers and worked for peace in Ireland. There are those who can accept pain and suffering and tragedy not only in their own lives, but in the lives of those near and dear to them, without as it were turning against God and suspending their belief in him: on the contrary this seems to bring God nearer to them, and through their pain they find joy. They compare their experience with Jesus's experience of forsakenness on the cross, and believe that it is through such experience that they can, like him, be brought to newness of life.

When an intellectual explanation of the evil and natural disasters in the world is sought, Christians have no compelling answer. They may attempt to show that such things must be allowed to happen, for if human beings are to be free to make choices, this freedom must be built into the evolving planet (giving rise to earthquakes, etc.), into the viruses and bacteria which infect human beings (as instanced in pain, suffering and tragic death) and into the constitution of human beings (giving rise to appalling crimes against people). Perhaps, if people accepted this explanation, there would be a greater value put upon human freedom. But the experience of suffering and the tragedy usually takes priority over such attempted explanations. The only way, I believe, that pain, suffering and injustice can be accepted is through the acknowledgement that God suffered the worst that human beings could do to him through the suffering and death of Jesus Christ; that Christ accepted this, and that suffering and death were turned into victory and new life through his resurrection; and that this experience of life through death is validated in our own experience of suffering, however horrible it may be. The symbol of the cross for me is a potent sign amid life's appalling tragedies because it is a sign that God cares, and can bring good out of evil. But I have to admit that for unbelievers it is just a beautiful symbol without the meaning I put upon it.

Intellectually speaking, there is no compelling reason for belief or unbelief either way. For my own part, I hold that the intellectual arguments in favour of belief are far the stronger, and that we are given a way through frightful tragedies of suffering and evil and disaster and the powerlessness that these bring; but I have to admit that not all would agree with me. It follows that I have failed to discover any compelling intellectual proof why people should believe or disbelieve the existence of God.

Can it be that this method is mistaken? Should we accept the Barthian premise of the total discontinuity between divine revelation and human striving after God? Such a view stems from the belief that fallen humanity is so steeped in sin that it is no longer made in God's image, and therefore it is only through the saving grace of Christ that God's truth can be revealed. The Word of God comes as it were vertically down into the heart, bringing within itself its own authenticity and authority. No: I cannot accept this approach. I cannot accept a faith unless it can be shown to be a rational choice. Barthianism suggests that belief in God should be confined only to Christians who experience the grace of Christ, whereas it is in fact found in all the great world religions. Once we distrust the power of human reason to find truth, we have no means of distinguishing between true and false revelation.

So what does really determine belief in God, if it cannot be conclusively demonstrated by rational argument? We might say that those who believe in God are more spiritually sensitive than others, but this would be somewhat arrogant. I have met agnostics who are very spiritually sensitive, far more sensitive than some Christians, but they find the evidence for God too ambiguous to commit themselves. I suspect that this ambiguity is intended by God, who wishes us to come to him by faith and not by sight; but there are others who regard it simply as a reflection of how things are.

It seems likely that unbelief is often caused by false ideas about the nature of God (and sometimes there may be personal moral reasons for it). As for those who continue in honest unbelief or agnosticism, if we believe that God is love and that 'God wills all men to be saved', we can rest assured that their future destiny is the most loving that God can give them.

As for faith in God, I think that it depends on a basic movement of the human heart: it is an interior conviction, a basic intuition, a fundamental insight; a 'blik', to use a word coined by Professor R. M. Hare. Those to whom this is given believe that arguments from the cosmos, the world and human personality are consonant with and support their belief in God; and they find it confirmed in experience and in the Scriptures. But it is not dependent on any of these. What causes this 'blik'? I do not think we can go further than describing it as a gift of God. Faith has traditionally been regarded as a divine gift: human beings cannot manufacture it. I would like to think that it is given to any who open themselves to receive it, but I realize that it would be too facile to assert that this is what always happens. Those who have it do not deserve it, but it is a gift which transforms their lives and fills them with love and peace and joy.

9

The Future of the Church

It is not my intention in this chapter to prophesy about the future of the Church. That depends on the future actions of men and women, and it is ultimately in the hands of God.

What follows is how, in my judgement, the Church ought to adapt itself in the future. It must always look towards the large number of people who are outside its confines, especially in times like today, when there is a spiritual vacuum, and when large numbers of people are searching for something which can give meaning to life and which can give them a relevant spirituality. As Archbishop William Temple is famously reported to have said, the Church is the only institution primarily concerned for those who are not its members. But at the moment the Church of England seems to be more and more self-concerned. As its numbers diminish, so it is increasingly concerned with its internal structures rather than with its message. For example the number of suffragan bishops has dramatically increased in a period when the number of worshippers has decreased. There is a plan to increase the number of people working for and with the Archbishop of Canterbury. It is a common complaint of Roman Catholics that their Church is overcentralized; and now the Church of England seems bent on increasing centralization, with activities recently put under the control of the Archbishops' Council. For example, in the days when I was chairman of the Church of England's Board for Social Responsibility, we had freedom to investigate and to speak out on any matter of social concern about which the Christian Church had something of importance to pronounce;

but nowadays permission is needed from above, from the Archbishops' Council, before such a matter may be taken up.

I can only speak about the Church of England; and here there seems an increased emphasis on 'orthodoxy'. For example, in the baptism service of the *Alternative Service Book* (which is no longer authorized for use) parents and godparents of a child to be baptized used to be asked two sets of three questions; whether they believed in God the Father who made the world, in God the Son who redeemed mankind, and God the Holy Spirit who gives life to the people of God. They were also asked whether they turned to Christ, repented of their sins and renounced evil; in other words whether they were disciples of Christ. But in the new *Common Worship* which has taken the place of the *Alternative Service Book*, the questions are different. There is an additional question, whether the parents and godparents reject the devil and rebellion against God. They are now not merely asked whether they believe in God the Father, Son and Holy Spirit: they are required to say that they believe every clause of the Apostles' Creed. (There is a simpler alternative for this, but even this is more theologically loaded than its equivalent in the *Alternative Service Book*, and it is only to be used 'where there are strong pastoral reasons' for so doing.) As a result of these changes, Christian orthodoxy seems to be replacing Christian discipleship as the main requirement in baptism. It is particularly strange that parents should be required to renounce the devil when comparatively few clergy believe that there is a personal devil to renounce. It is even stranger that they are required to believe every clause of the Apostles' Creed (including the virgin birth and the second advent) when many – perhaps most – of those who administer baptism do not themselves believe these doctrines! There is no indication in the liturgy that parents and godparents may legitimately hold these doctrines symbolically rather than literally.

I am not advocating that the Church of England should

abandon catholicity, and substitute instead formulations in its liturgies which are more liberal. There will always be those who tend towards fundamentalism and who insist on traditional credal orthodoxy, especially when the uncertainty of the times in which we live inclines people to seek rock-hard certainties in religion. Such people have a rightful place within the Church of England. Catholicity requires that they should continue to have an honoured position in the Church, and it would be as wrong to sideline them as it would be to ignore those who are equally committed to the Christian faith but who cannot conscientiously accept all orthodox formulations. Such people are sincerely Christian, but they understand their Christianity in terms more of Christian discipleship than Christian orthodoxy. All those who follow Christ should be able to join together in Christian fellowship, and that includes Catholics and Protestants, orthodox and liberals. I therefore regret the absence of alternatives in the liturgy for those who opt more for Christian discipleship. In an earlier chapter I have suggested that there be an optional alternative credal statement for use in place of the Nicene Creed. Similarly, at baptism I would make a plea for alternatives to be used for questions to the parents and godparents in *Common Worship*, not merely 'for strong pastoral reasons', but for the many, perhaps the majority of cases when parents who wish their children to be brought up as Christians are themselves theologically illiterate. They are more concerned with orthopraxy – right conduct – than with the minutiae of orthodoxy. In our emphasis on orthodoxy we have, I fear, over-intellectualized Christianity. This is, I think, the special danger of a Church whose principal reformer was a former Cambridge don, Thomas Cranmer.

It is all the more necessary to allow for such alterations because of the present situation in which the Church finds itself. Most people nowadays have little knowledge of Christianity. It seems to them to be a prescientific, outdated and arcane sort of religion, and its credal formulations appear to be a lot of mumbo-jumbo. This may be somewhat crudely put, but a sharp reminder is needed to indicate how far removed the Church is from the thought forms of many contemporary people, especially the unsophisticated. In a materialistic culture, where scientific explanations rule the day, people find it hard to accept the miraculous supernaturalism in which orthodox Christianity has been traditionally expressed. And yet they are looking for a meaning to life and a form of spirituality suited to their needs. A simple but sincere faith in God, and an equally sincere and simple faith in Jesus as expressing the nature of God in terms of human personality – that they can understand. The teaching of Jesus, as expressed in the Sermon on the Mount and elsewhere in the Gospels – that is a challenge they can also understand. When such teaching and such a faith is matched by the quality of life of those who are already Christians – that they can appreciate. Even though reunion of the Churches is impossible, fraternal relations between them should be full of the same Christian love and understanding as should exist between individual Christians – that could speak volumes. Tolerance of other religions and respect for the faith of their adherents, without the surrender of Christian convictions – that also is likely to commend Christianity. A Church which can make its way on its own spiritual dynamic, divested of the trappings of the Establishment, is more likely to appeal to the hearts of those at present outside the Church than a body established by law and connected with those in political power. These are the challenges which the Church faces today.

Young people, in particular, find little in the present-day Church of England which satisfies them spiritually. They can hardly be expected to be over-enthusiastic about services which are overwhelmingly attended by the middle-aged and the elderly. They need something more suited to the culture of their age-group. For this reason Youth Festivals such as Greenbelt are excellent in their ability to speak to young people with colour and music and in language suited to their culture. Without young people today, where will the Church be when they grow up? More Youth Festivals of this informal kind should be encouraged both nationally and at local level.

These suggestions are not intended to result in a watering down of the Church's faith. In particular the shape of the Eucharist, the main service of the Church, must remain unchanged, even though alternatives such as I have suggested should be permitted. The incarnation, the passion and death of Christ, the resurrection, and the outpouring of the Holy Spirit are key events in the Christian story and must be celebrated in worship in the traditional way. But it must be borne in mind that it is not teaching about Jesus but the story of Jesus that is at the centre of the Christian faith.

Nor do I suggest for a moment that the Church should dispense with its sacraments, its Scriptures, its calendar, the historic episcopate, and other marks of its catholicity, although I do suggest that, if these are to be generally acceptable to the vast majority of the unchurched, it is necessary not to make inflated claims on their behalf. There is certainly inspiration in biblical writings, but that does not mean that everything in the Bible is inspired, still less that infallibility should be ascribed to all its contents. The sacraments are a wonderful means of grace, but that does not mean that miraculous changes take place when certain verbal formulae are said over them: they function mostly by means of symbolism. Baptism makes a child a member of the Church; but that does not mean that pouring water on a baby in the name of the Trinity automatically washes away its inheritance of self-centredness. Christian marriage is intended to be lifelong; but that does not mean that when a marriage tragically dies, the divorced partners must never remarry. The historic episcopate marks the continuity of the Church down the centuries, but that does not mean that it is of the essence of the Church. God's gifts to his Church are to be cherished and honoured, but they lose credibility if we make them appear supernatural and miraculous.

If the Church is the one institution primarily concerned with those who are not its members, the question must be asked – when does it meet those who are not its members? In one sense it meets them all the time, whenever non-Christians meet a Christian. But when do formal meetings between the Church and non-Christians take place? This happens for the most part at what are known as 'the occasional offices': baptism, confirmation, marriage and especially funerals. Those are the occasions when non-Christians attend Christian worship, as friends or relatives of those to be baptized, confirmed or married, and particularly of those who have died. It is especially important that these liturgies should be readily understood by the non-Christians present, and that sermons or addresses that are given should appeal to their imagination and be relevant to their understanding. A certain informality, compatible with the dignity of Anglican worship, is called for on these occasions.

There are other occasions, often through the mass media, when a broader audience can be addressed. Christians should be careful not to make triumphalist claims for their faith, but to point out the ambiguities to be faced when considering the existence of God, ambiguities which can only be overcome by the God-given gift of faith rather than by rational arguments, which at best can only lead to probabilities. At the same time the Christian faith needs to be defended against atheist attacks, and the Church badly needs lay journalists who can use their skills in its defence. Scientists who are Christians are needed to parry the attacks of their non-believing colleagues who seem to take delight in using their literary talents to denigrate quite unfairly the Christian faith: few people outside the Church seem to realize just how favourable contemporary scientific knowledge is to the claims of Christianity.

Even more important is the voice of the Church over the

moral aspect of many contemporary social issues. This is where the reports of the Board for Social Responsibility and the voice of its chairman ought to be heard. The Roman Catholic Church is to be congratulated on the development of its work in this field, for example in its report *The Common Good*. There are many issues of modern medical technology that need to be addressed, especially those concerning fertilization and death. Genetic engineering cries aloud for an authoritative assessment by the Church. The dangers of chemical and biological weapons need to be addressed. The Church ought to campaign strongly for sustainable development, for this is God's world, and we have no right to wreck it. Among the billions of stars in the billions of galaxies in our universe, this planet may well be the only one which supports life, and in which life has evolved. It would be very terrible if humankind through greed and thoughtlessness threatened the future of our planet.

There are other social issues about which the Church should concern itself. Major questions concerning the principles underlying new proposals over state secondary education need probing from a Christian point of view. Matters concerning the use of private enterprise in public institutions (PPP) need moral exploration. The moral aspects of globalization need examining. Guidance is needed on the moral aspects of new scientific discoveries and technological innovation. If the Church were to voice its concerns on these matters, and give spiritual and moral guidance concerning them, it would be seen by the world at large to have a message relevant to ordinary people. The word 'theology' is now often loosely used to describe theorizing that has no practical import. But if the Church were to show its concern for the moral and spiritual aspects of these matters, it would be seen to have a message that is relevant not merely for the private lives of individuals, but also for the great issues that now face humankind, and this would greatly increase its credibility among the many unchurched in our country.

There would not be sufficient expertise among the staff of the Archbishops' Council's Board for Social Responsibility to deal with most of these questions, but there is a great deal of goodwill among experts, many of whom are Christians, who would be willing to form working parties to consider many of these subjects. Their expenses of travel would not be inconsiderable, but it would be money well spent, not merely because the impartial voice of the Church is needed in a climate of prejudice, experience and sound-bites, and because the moral and spiritual aspects of these matters badly need to be explored, but also because to do so would greatly advance the mission of the Church.

Would it be possible for the Church to advance along the lines suggested in this chapter? Is the Church so bound to its traditional ways that it is merely fanciful to make these suggestions? It would certainly be the case with some Churches. But the Church of England was set up on a broad base in order to embrace all English people. In this it failed. But the broad base remains. Providing that the position of traditionalists (whether Catholic or Protestant) is guaranteed, so that they can continue as they have done in the past, this should be possible. The Church has been able to make progress by producing contemporary worship, and at the same time retaining the Book of Common Prayer as an option for those who wish to use it. The Church has been able to ordain women to the priesthood and at the same time to retain the loyalty of those who object to this by means of 'flying bishops' and by allowing them to refuse the ministry of women priests in their parish church, if such is their request. In the same kind of way, it would be possible to allow alternative credal formulae and alternative questions for the baptism of infants, and to take other steps to meet the needs of those who are committed Christians but who cannot accept in good conscience all the traditional doctrines of the Church (and perhaps cannot even understand them). It might even be possible to state that while these doctrines always have an important symbolic value, they need not all be taken literally by all members of the Church. For example, those who find it hard to accept that Jesus was born of a virgin can find profound spiritual value in its symbolic value as marking a new start for the human race, just as the second advent of Christ, for those who cannot take it literally, can have a deep symbolic value as marking the completion of God's purposes for this world.

The time has passed when it is possible to persuade the population at large of the truth of Christian doctrine in traditional and literal terms. We have moved into a new era of civilization, and the new era calls for a new paradigm of the Christian faith which respects and values the beliefs of other faiths without jeopardizing its own uniqueness. In today's world, for all its scientific and technological advances, and for all its modern glitz and hype, there is a spiritual vacuum which could be filled by a Christian faith which retains the kernel of the gospel but which has adapted itself in the kind of ways suggested here. Instead of acquiescing with a continuing drop in its numbers, the Church of England could commend itself to the many who are hungry and thirsty for a spirituality that is meaningful for their lives.

There is hope for the future of the Church of England. The upkeep of its ancient churches (which are an important part of the nation's heritage) is an enormous burden of which it must be relieved. Despite the bad press it receives in the mass media, it still has a firm base. Many more have been recently found to be attending its churches than was thought. It was recently stated in the Roman Catholic *Tablet* (I mention its affiliation to show that this is not a triumphalist Anglican claim) that three out of four people said that they were Christian, and that half of these said they were Church of England. Doubtless many only meant that they would like to be buried by its ministry, but it shows at the very least the goodwill it retains. There is no anticlericalism. Its church schools are enormously popular, among church people and the unchurched alike.

Affluence and consumerism had certainly affected the Church at the end of the last century, and perhaps it will not achieve full strength until it has endured the kind of harassment and persecution which Christians of Eastern European countries had to face under Communism, and experienced the resurrection that comes through sharing in Christ's sense of forsakenness on the cross. But it is regaining lost morale. It needs a prophet at its helm, courage to meet the challenges of the present day, and Christian discipleship and spirituality to be valued above religious orthodoxy.

References

Ad Gentes in S. Abbott (ed.), *The Documents of Vatican II.* Chapman, 1966.

Avis, P., *Church, State and Establishment.* SPCK, 2001.

Best, E. *One Body in Christ.* SPCK, 1955.

Bethune-Baker, J. F., *The Early History of the Christian Church,* Lutterworth, 1961.

Bosch, D. J., *Transforming Mission.* Orbis, 1991.

Buchanan, C., *Cut the Connection.* Darton, Longman & Todd, 1994.

Catechism of the Catholic Church. Chapman, 1994.

Chadwick, W. O., *The Victorian Church.* Cambridge University Press, 1972.

Cohn-Sherbok, D., *The Crucified Jew.* HarperCollins, 1992.

Common Good, The: statement by the Catholic Bishops' Conference of England and Wales, 1996.

Congregation for the Doctrine of the Faith, *Dominus Iesus.* CTS, 2001.

Crick, F., *Life Itself.* Simon & Schuster, 1981.

Cullmann, O., *The Christology of the New Testament.* SCM Press, 1959.

Dawkins, R., *The Blind Watchmaker.* Longmans, 1986.

Desmond, A. and Moore, J., *Darwin.* Penguin, 1992.

Dunn, J. D. G., *Unity and Diversity in the New Testament.* SCM Press, 1977.

Fieldsend, J., *Messianic Jews.* Monarch Publications, 1993.

Fisher, E., 'Why Convert the Saved?', *The Tablet* (14 July 2001).

References

Franklin, R. M. (ed.), *Apostolicae Curae*. Mowbray, 1996.

Garbett, C., *Church and State in England*. Hodder & Stoughton, 1959.

Gould, S. J., *Wonderful Life*. Penguin, 1989.

Gregorios *et al.*, *Does Chalcedon Divide or Unite?* World Council of Churches, 1981.

Hadfield, P., 'Nukes in the Basement', *New Scientist* (25 August 2001).

Hick, J., *An Interpretation of Religion*. Macmillan, 1989.

Interchurch House, *Christians and Jews: A New Way of Thinking*, 1994.

Ipgrave, M. (ed.), *Sharing One Hope?* Church House Publishing, 2001.

John Paul II, *Redemptoris Missio*, Encyclical Letter, 1990.

Küng, H., *Judaism*. SCM Press, 1992.

Küng, H., *Christianity and the World Religions*. SCM Press, 1993.

Leitzmann, H., *A History of the Early Church*. Lutterworth, 1961.

Lomborg, B., *The Skeptical Environmentalist*. Cambridge University Press, 2001.

Lovelock, J. W., *Gaia*. Oxford University Press, 1979.

Lovelock, J. W., *The Science of Planetary Medicine*. Gaia Books, 1991.

McLaren, D., *et al.*, *Tomorrow's World*. Earthscan, 1998.

Montefiore, H., 'Christology for Today', *Soundings*, ed. A. Vidler. Cambridge University Press, 1963.

Montefiore, H., *The Question Mark: The End of Homo Sapiens*. Collins, 1969.

Montefiore, H., *The Probability of God*. SCM Press, 1985.

Montefiore, H., *Credible Christianity*. Mowbrays, 1993.

Moorman, J. R. G., *A History of the Church of England*. Black, 1953.

References

Nostra Aetate in S. Abbott (ed.), *Documents of Vatican II*. Chapman, 1966.

Parkes, J., *Conflict of the Church and Synagogue*. Soncino Press, 1934.

Penrose, R., *et al.*, *The Large, the Small and the Human Mind*. Cambridge University Press, 1997.

Ratcliffe, E., *The Coronation Service of Queen Elizabeth II*. SPCK, 1953.

Rees, M., *Our Cosmic Habitat*. Weidenfeld & Nicolson, 2002.

Robinson, J. A. T., *The Body*. SCM Press, 1952.

Romain, J. A., *Your God Shall Be My God*. SCM Press, 2000.

Stevenson, I., *Reincarnation and Biology*. Praeger, 1997a.

Stevenson, I., *Where Reincarnation and Biology Intersect*. Praeger, 1997b.

Taylor, S. R., 'On the Difficulties of Earth-like Planets', *Meteoritics and Planetary Science*, 1999.

Underhill, E., *Mysticism*. Methuen, 1923.

Unitatis Redintegratio in S. Abbott, (ed.), *Documents of Vatican II*. Chapman, 1966.

Wilson, A. N., *God's Funeral*. Murray, 1999.